COUNSELING THE ELDERLY
A Systems Approach

James F. Keller
and
George A. Hughston

VIRGINIA POLYTECHNIC
INSTITUTE
AND STATE UNIVERSITY

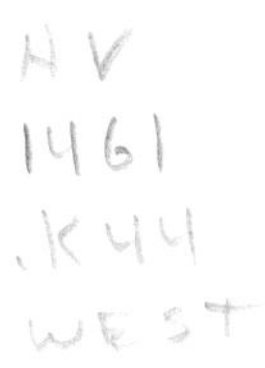

HARPER & ROW, PUBLISHERS, New York
Cambridge, Hagerstown, Philadelphia, San Francisco,
London, Mexico City, São Paulo, Sydney

Sponsoring Editor: Alan Spiegel
Production Manager: Jeanie Berke
Compositor: Maryland Linotype Composition Co., Inc.
Printer and Binder: The Murray Printing Company

Counseling the Elderly A Systems Approach

Library of Congress Cataloging in Publication Data

Keller, James F   Date–
Counseling the elderly.

Includes bibliographical references and index.
1. Social work with the aged—United States.
2. Aged—Care and hygiene. 3. Counseling—United States. I. Hughston, George A., joint author.
II. Title.
HV1461.K44   362.6   80–23709
ISBN 0–06–453511–8

Contents

Preface

This book represents an attempt at incorporating the numerous strategies for psychological intervention with older persons in a focused theoretical model. There is a notable absence in the literature of counseling theories with primary attention on the later years. Attempts at relating therapeutically with older persons have ranged from as little preparation as simple sincerity to uneasy translations of approaches more easily adapted to younger persons. Obviously, we do not have the final word. The presentation may at times sound as if we feel that way. We are optimistic and excited about the approach, but in our most rational moments we are confident that this book is only a first step from which it is hoped that new ideas and methods will emerge. We would like to encourage you to challenge the material presented and to develop creative new ways to enable the elderly not only to cope with life's problems but to enjoy life right up to the end.

Undergraduates and beginning graduate students involved in human development and professional programs will find the counseling model useful, especially in applied areas of their study. A special effort has been made to give enough theory to facilitate the establishment of guidelines for situations that will arise where there might be little prior experience.

The book suggests a need for attitude change with those of us who counsel the aged. The potential for constructive coping with aging is often eroded by our good intentions, which come across as feeling sorry for, expecting little of, and taking responsibility for the elderly. In addition, a psychological intervention approach like the one we are proposing presupposes an understanding of demographic trends and physiological developments in the aging years. Various encouragement strategies and techniques are presented with case study examples. These vignettes represent case histories of actual experiences with elderly individuals. They have been shortened in most cases with enough details changed to protect confidentiality.

Special appreciation is expressed to our families, who gave encouragement by enduring us throughout the project, and to the elderly, who continue to inspire us by pushing back the threshold of independent living.

Special thanks are also due Sheldon Gelman of The Pennsylvania State University, Mary O'Day of the University of California at Berkeley, Robert Morris of Brandeis University, Art Farber of the University of Washington, and Mel Markorvski of East Carolina University for their intensive readings and important suggestions for revisions. Many of their contributions were incorporated in the final draft. Last, but not least, we are indebted to Mrs. Lewis Whitescarver for her patient and persistent typing of the revisions and the final draft.

George A. Hughston
James F. Keller

Chapter 1
Trends and Numbers

Before a systematic approach for psychological intervention with older persons can be developed, it is important to understand the issue of aging within a historical context. One is tempted either to underplay or to exaggerate a social problem when it is considered outside the parameters of history.

Further, it is imperative that the demographic boundaries of the aging population be established. To know the dimensions of the social problem is to proceed, with knowledge, toward a more reasonable solution.

HISTORICAL TRENDS

Simone de Beauvoir (1972) has cataloged the long history of societal attitudes toward aging. For our purposes we will highlight historical developments in a brief summary from her exhaustive survey. She pointed out that it was Hippocrates (460–377 B.C.) who made one of the first contributions toward an understanding of aging: comparing human life with nature's four seasons (birth to spring, aging to winter, etc.). In addition, his book *Aphorisms* detailed physical ailments suffered in the later years: respiratory problems, joint pains, painful urination, kidney diseases, vertigo, apoplexy, cachexia, and so on. One of his major conclusions some 2400 years ago was: *The aged should not stop working at their jobs.* In its own way, this was a kind of intervention strategy. Maintaining a job responsibility is more likely to communicate a sense of being needed and valued. This feeling of continued contribution translates into greater personal and emotional health.

Aristotle's (384–322 B.C.) discussion of aging concluded that the body's internal heat was the necessary condition of life. Galen (130–200 A.D.), a Greek physician and writer, developed a synthesis of the ideas of Hippocrates and Aristotle. His conclusion: Old age was something lying between illness and health. One unique conclusion that we wish to emphasize from this historical sketch so far is that *prevention* of deterioration rather than *cure* became identified with the medical approach to aging. The preventive model recommended hot baths, wine drinking, and *remaining active.* For centuries Galen's views of preserving independence of older persons prevailed. The Church Fathers adopted his synthesis and no basic alterations were made in the approach during the Middle Ages. For centuries the predominant societal posture toward aging was to support continued activity and involvement. This heritage is worth recalling in this twentieth century so characterized by societal attitudes of limiting involvement of older individuals.

We can see the historical roots of this twentieth-century malady. Gradually aging began to be seen in terms of pathology. Roger Bacon (1214–1294) identified age as a disease. This approach is certainly not to be viewed as all negative. Many good things came of it: Magnifying lenses were offered to correct poor sight; false teeth, obtained from animals and human "baby" teeth, were introduced. By the fifteenth century hygiene becomes the predominant focus of interest in aging. Zerbi published *Gerontocomia* in this period. It was the first book to be devoted to the pathology of old age.

During the Renaissance, anatomical studies related to aging made advances even though they were still steeped in metaphysics. The dissection of human bodies had been long forbidden, but by the end of the fifteenth century it became possible, with Leonardo de Vinci generally seen as the founder. Paracelsus (1493–1591) struck out in new directions, concluding that a human being was a chemical compound, with age brought on by autointoxication. The trend was set by this time. It was Gerard Van Swieten in the seventeenth century who concluded that old age is an incurable disease. This pattern brought both fortunate and unfortunate implications. Remedies and corrective approaches spawned by the developing "medical model" of aging brought much relief to nagging problems of decline. The unfortunate by-product was a developing attitude of aging as a disease that was handled by *doing for* the old. This view emphasizes the problems of aging and shifts the focus away from the *resources* and *potential* of older people for prevention of early deterioration.

The decline in metaphysical influences on the study of science is seen in the increasing interest, in this period, in the combination of physics and biology in the study of aging. The body was seen as a machine with cylinders, spindles, and wheels. Lungs were compared with bellows. Aging meant that the body, like machines, wears out when used too long. This view enjoyed its greatest popularity in the late eighteenth and nineteenth centuries. Stahl proposed that humans contained within themselves a vital principle, an entity. The weakening of this principle, through wear, brings about old age and its disappearance, death.

Large institutions housing many old people were established in France in the nineteenth century. Charcot, Freud's mentor, gave his famous lectures on aging at Salpetriere, the largest institution in Europe housing old people. The significant trend development in this historical period is the move away from a preventive approach to aging to one of cure. Examples include a 72-year-old professor in France, Brown-Siguard, who injected himself with an extract of testicles from guinea pigs and dogs to "cure" his aging process. No lasting results were reported. By the twentieth century age was seen in terms of artery condition; that is, it was related to the presence of atherosclerosis. Generally, by the beginning of the twentieth century, the study of the aging process was a by-product of other research, for example, the study of anatomy, alteration of plants as they grow older, and so on.

Since the last half of the nineteenth century significant changes in the role and status of the elderly in society have been detected. The transition involves the meaning of old age (Achenbaum, 1979). There is a gradual shift for the elderly from a more positive constructive role to a more negative displaced position in American life. It becomes more difficult to find examples in literature after 1865 that associate physical and mental skills with elderly persons.

The fact that the number of older persons doubled between 1900 and 1930 and again between 1930 and 1950 prompted the direct study of aging for the first time. The initial studies (late nineteenth and early twentieth century) had focused on only the defective aspects of older persons. Later studies polarized around aging as a continuing process, as part of developmental psychology. Current issues of study in aging include DNA-RNA research with attempts to determine why cells age for the purpose of exploring the possibility of chemically deterring the aging process. With the very recent interest in research for determining the potential of older persons for independence in their later years, we may be at the threshold of a significant period in the study of aging. Ironically, we may be just beginning to return to the wisdom of our ancestors. The economic predicament of this period is forcing the development of a philosophy more compatible with the nurturance of the resources of the elderly themselves. The increasing number of older people is having more of an impact. There are some signs of growing influence from the organization of their numbers into political power blocs (e.g., Senior Power, American Association of Retired Persons, Gray Panthers). As the number of older persons increases, their needs and concerns will have to be taken more seriously.

Historically, different ages had different values and interests with regard to the problems of elderly individuals. Some societies in early periods saw aging in more positive terms and valued continued vocational activity well into the later years. With the accumulation of results from specialized scientific knowledge, today a more optimistic view is emerging concerning the abilities and potential of the aged. For the first time there is scientific support for gains in abilities that may extend throughout the life span. Difficulties remain, however. A major problem for the study of aging in the twentieth century will continue to be the collection of accurate research data. An additional challenge is the dissemination of these research results. The century-old negative myths about aging die hard.

POPULATION STATISTICS OF OLDER AMERICANS

A major assumption of this book is that psychological intervention with older persons must be grounded in a knowledge of the characteristics of individuals in this age category and an understanding of the aging process. To develop a base for counseling older persons, an overview of the most recent data with respect to older persons is essential. The social trends and conditions, as reflected in census data, may provide clues for the directions independence development may take in the later years.

Within the United States dramatic changes are occurring in the statistical proportion of elderly in the population. In absolute number, in 1950 there were 12.4 million Americans over 65. This number had jumped to 20.1 million in 1970 and by 1977 census data reveal there were over 22.9 million Americans age 65 plus (Table 1–1). Since the birthrate in the United States began to declne in the 1970s the population makeup has shifted. Demographers predict that by 1980 at least 24.5 million people will be over 65 years of age and by 1990 this number will have grown to 29.8 million. By the year 2000 it is predicted that there will be 31.8 million elderly in this country.

Table 1–1 ESTIMATED AND PROJECTED POPULATION, BY AGE AND SEX, 1950 TO 2000
(figures are in thousands)

Year	Population 65 years and over	Females 65 years and over	Males 65 years and over
1950	12,397	6,541	5,856
1960	16,675	9,133	47,542
1970	20,087	11,681	8,407
1975	22,405	13,228	9,176
1976	22,934	13,571	9,364
1980	24,927	14,819	10,108
1985	27,305	16,293	11,612
1990	29,824	17,824	11,999
2000	31,822	19,105	12,717

SOURCE: U.S. Bureau of the Census, 1977.

Although the rising numbers of older people are of critical interest to society, it is *not* the absolute numbers of old people that are most significant; it is the *proportion* of older people in relation to the rest of the population. This proportion has been increasing at a rapid pace. In 1900, 4.1 percent of the population was 65 and over. In 50 years this proportion has doubled (8.1 percent). It is expected to double again in approximately 80 years.

These increases are being hastened by declining birthrates. In 1955, the U.S. birthrate rose to a level of 25.0 births per 1000 population, the highest since before World War II. By 1960 this rate had declined to 23.7 and fell even further to 14.9 in 1973. The years of 1970 and 1973 represent the lowest rates in the United States since the turn of the century.

The rising proportion of older persons and the projected increases (Table 1–1), in the population have potential for many far-reaching implications. Increased political and social influence will certainly evolve as this proportion of the population increases. More control over legislation and increased power for affecting the nation's priorities and values seem certain to evolve as this country moves closer to a nation of older people.

The increased proportion of older persons 65 and over will mean greater strains on the national budget. A shrinking number of younger people will be financing an increasing number of older persons. The ratio of wage earners to pensioners in the U.S. social security system was 35 to 1 in 1945. In 1976 the ratio had fallen to 3.2 to 1.

The opportunity of older persons to continue to support themselves has also been severely limited. It is almost forgotten that in 1900 that proportion of males who were still in the labor force beyond 65 years of age was 70 percent. In 1950 the figure had dropped to 50 percent, 30 percent in 1960, and only 14 percent in 1976. The automatic retirement at 65, and the limitations placed on earning while receiving social security payments prevent older persons from assuming more economic responsibility for their own lives. But, in the short term, there would be real problems finding enough jobs for those individuals over 65 who would choose to continue to work. In the long term, as birthrates continue to decline and the proportion of the population swings toward a larger older population, there may well be a greater dependence on the older population to supply the services needed. When the first generations born during our declining-birthrate years approach retirement, there will not be inflated numbers of new workers flooding into the labor force to take their places. When this occurs, employers may find themselves enticing employees to stay on the job beyond regular retirement ages. With the elderly assuming more responsibility for themselves, their own independence is reinforced, both psychologically and economically. The strains on federal support resources would let up as well. Until this long-term trend appears, however, the burden will be with us.

The economic strains have begun to appear. Already surfacing in the news media, reports are questioning how long the social security system can remain solvent under the duress of the many to be supported by the few. This stress is coming at a time when even with government support one-sixth of all older Americans 65 or over are living below the poverty line. The current figures are depressing and misleading, but the decade trend is hopeful. The figure for *all* persons over 65 below the poverty line masks significant racial differences. In 1959, 35 percent of all those over 65 were below the poverty line (this figure included 62 percent of blacks over 65 and 33 percent of whites), whereas in 1969 the overall level has dropped to 25 percent (50.5 percent of blacks over 65 and 23 percent of whites). In the latest year of completed statistics the level had dropped in 1974 to 16 percent over all (36.4 percent of blacks and 14 percent of whites over 65). (*Newsweek*, Feb. 28, 1977; USDC, Series P–23, No. 57, p. 37, 1974). Although it is certainly dismaying to have one-sixth of all older Americans in this category, the downward trend in the proportion of older Americans below the poverty line is certainly encouraging. For the 16 percent of Americans still below the line a continued concerted effort toward alleviating this problem is essential. This is particularly important in view of recent high levels of inflation in the very areas that affect older people most: rent, utilities, and medical care. A government, if it survives, has no choice in *whether* it will support its older citizens. A dilemma exists, however. Younger wage earners who must pay larger and larger shares of the support program may develop increasingly hostile postures toward the aged. But even greater national problems will exist if the support is not forthcoming. The 1971 White House Conference on Aging stated, "There is no substitute for income if people are to be free to exercise choices in their style of living. . . . Only when their incomes are adequate and secure can the aged be expected to lead meaningful, self-respecting, and independent lives" (Section Recommendations on Income, 1971 White House Conference on Aging. Washington, D.C.: Government Printing Office, 1972, pp. 1, 12).

The magnitude of growing economic costs may be enough to bring about changes in our national approach toward the independence of older persons. It seems increasingly clear that the government's traditional structures for bearing the financial burden of its elderly are under great strain. It also seems clear that a government cannot afford not to support its old people. However this dilemma is addressed and solved, it seems logical that development toward greater independence would be a part of it. A national program aimed at increasing the independence of the elderly may be one of the few viable options that a government can afford. It is ironic that we should be forced by economic pressures into a national concern that has the potential for giving older persons a greater sense of self-reliance and continued enrichment. Old people themselves cannot afford the drain of self-confidence and loss of individual integrity that come from "dependency-oriented" programs. It should not be forgotten that an increasing number of citizens who experience greater independence represents an untapped national resource.

LIFE SPAN AVERAGES

The current figures on life span expectancy tell us just about how long, after the "magic" year of retirement, that some support-independence system will be needed for the average American. This life span of the average American has steadily increased. In 1920 the average white American male could expect to live to be 54.4 years old, while his female counterpart could plan on 55.6 years, a difference of 1.2 years. By 1940 the average life span had jumped to 62.1 years for the white male and 66.6 years for the white female, a 4.5-year difference. Census data for 1975 reveal that the average white American male will live to be 69.4 years old, whereas the white female, on the average, reaches the ripe old age of 77.2 years, a 7.8-year difference. Generally, black Americans have shorter life spans than whites (Table 1–2), but as among whites, the black female outlives the black male. Life span averages for black and white males have increased very little since 1955, while both black and white female averages have been steadily rising.

The expanding gap in life span expectancy between males and females means that marriage for most females can be said to be "prepa-

Table 1–2 EXPECTATION OF LIFE[a] EXPECTATION OF LIFE AT BIRTH: 1920–1975

	Total			White			Negro and Other		
Year	Total	Male	Female	Total	Male	Female	Total	Male	Female
1920	54.1	53.6	54.6	54.9	54.4	55.6	45.3	45.5	45.2
1930	59.7	58.1	61.6	61.4	59.7	63.5	48.1	47.3	49.2
1940	62.9	60.8	65.2	64.2	62.1	66.6	53.1	51.5	54.9
1950	68.2	65.6	71.1	69.1	66.5	72.2	60.8	59.1	62.9
1955	69.6	66.7	72.8	70.5	67.4	73.7	63.7	61.4	66.1
1960	69.7	66.6	73.1	70.6	67.4	74.1	63.6	61.1	66.3
1965	70.2	66.8	73.7	71.0	67.6	74.7	64.1	61.1	67.4
1970	70.9	67.1	74.8	71.7	68.0	75.6	65.3	61.3	69.4
1971	71.1	67.4	75.0	72.0	68.3	75.8	65.6	61.6	69.7
1972	71.1	67.4	75.1	72.0	68.3	75.9	65.6	61.5	69.9
1973	71.3	67.6	75.3	72.2	68.4	76.1	65.9	61.9	70.1
1974	71.9	68.1	75.8	72.7	68.9	76.6	67.0	62.9	71.3
1975	72.5	68.7	76.5	73.2	69.4	77.2	67.9	63.6	72.3

SOURCE: U.S. National Center for Health Statistics. *Vital Statistics of the United States*, 1977.
[a] In years. Prior to 1960 these figures exclude Alaska and Hawaii. Data prior to 1940 for death-registration States only; see text. Se also *Historical Statistics, Colonial Times to 1970*, series B, 107–115.

ration for widowhood." This is not meant to ignore the number of men living without their spouses (Table 1–3). Even Plato (427–347 B.C.) was aware of the significantly higher number of widows than widowers and suggested that males marry older females. The ever-present phenomena of powerful social psychological forces have kept men, generally, coupled with younger females. In 1975, there were 144 women to every 100 males 65 years and older, whereas 40 years ago the ratio was about even. It is estimated that by the year 2000 the figures will have risen to about 154 females for every 100 males (Hendricks & Hendricks, 1979). In a culture that values marriage the trend toward increasing numbers of women living out their later years alone will be a problem related to increasing independence.

Cardiovascular problems and cancer deal men as a group a heavy blow during the later years. Although little accurate speculation has been made concerning the causes of cancer, much has been written about the factors that contribute to heart attacks and other cardiovascular difficulties. It appears that *many* factors may be responsible for cardiovascular decline. Some of the most frequently mentioned causes include diet, social pressures, lack of exercise, genetic background, exposure to pollutants (such as coal dust or smoking), and stress. Amount of stress may be directly connected to increased heart-related difficulties.

With the increasing professional involvement of women and the accompanying pressures and stresses that have been so graphically related to cardiovascular problems, future statistics may see a modification of the differences in the death rate between the sexes.

AGE AND SEX ROLE TRENDS

Some of the problems of aging are directly related to the kind of sex role preparation that is received as children and reinforced at all age stages in our culture. For example, young male children get the message that their goal in life in primarily career-oriented, and with this orientation the impact of the consequent instrumental responsibility for the family gradually pervades their mentality. Males learn early that they must "achieve" to establish their worth. They must be strong and not cry. Females are still raised in most families today to look toward a future with marriage and family as their primary goal. There has been a lot of talk about equality between the sexes, but still very little actual movement has occurred. The U.S. Census's 1976 *Statistical Portrait of Women* reported more women working than ever before, but more than half were employed in clerical, operative, or service positions. The proportion was actually higher in 1970 (48 percent) than in 1960 (43 percent). In 1970, 30 percent of males and 2 per-

Table 1–3 PERSONS 65 YEARS OLD AND OVER—CHARACTERISTICS, BY SEX: 1960 TO 1976

Item		1960		1965		1970		1975		1976	
		Male	Female	Male	Female	Male	Female	Male	Female	Male	Female
Total	(millions)	7.5	9.0	7.9	10.2	8.3	11.5	8.7	12.4	8.9	12.7
Percentage of total population		8.6	9.9	8.4	10.3	8.5	11.1	8.6	11.5	8.7	11.7
White	(millions)	6.9	8.4	7.3	9.4	7.6	10.6	7.9	11.3	8.0	11.6
Black	(millions)	0.5	0.6	0.6	0.8	0.7	0.9	0.8	1.1	0.9	1.1
Age:											
65–69 years	(percent)	3.3	3.7	3.1	3.6	3.2	3.7	3.5	4.1	3.5	4.2
70–74 years	(percent)	2.5	2.8	2.5	3.0	2.3	3.0	2.4	3.0	2.4	3.1
75–79 years	(percent)	1.5	1.9	1.6	2.0	1.6	2.2	1.5	2.2	1.5	2.2
80 years and over	(percent)	1.2	1.6	1.3	1.9	1.4	2.3	1.5	2.7	1.5	2.8
Median income:											
Families	(dollars)	(NA)	(NA)	(NA)	(NA)	4,779	4,986	7,469	7,722	8,023	8,311
Unrelated individuals	(dollars)	(NA)	(NA)	(NA)	(NA)	2,191	1,777	3,410	2,901	3,692	3,235
Percent below poverty level:											
Family heads		29.7	31.5	22.4	27.0	16.6	23.5	7.9	12.3	8.3	12.7
Unrelated individuals		58.5	69.1	49.6	64.8	40.0	49.9	25.8	31.7	27.7	31.9
Percent distribution		100.0	100.0	100.0	100.0	100.0	100.0	100.0	100.0	100.0	100.0

Marital status:										
Single	7.3	8.5	6.6	7.7	7.5	7.7	4.7	5.8	4.4	5.9
Married	71.7	36.8	71.3	36.0	73.1	35.6	79.3	39.1	79.1	38.5
Spouse present	69.0	35.0	67.9	34.1	69.9	33.9	77.3	37.6	76.5	36.7
Spouse absent	2.7	1.8	3.4	1.9	3.2	1.7	2.0	1.5	2.6	1.8
Widowed	19.4	53.1	19.5	54.4	17.1	54.4	13.6	52.5	13.8	52.8
Divorced	1.7	1.5	2.6	1.9	2.3	2.3	2.5	2.6	2.7	2.8
Family status:										
In families	82.3	67.7	80.3	62.9	79.2	58.5	83.3	59.3	83.4	57.9
Primary individuals	12.8	26.8	13.9	30.6	14.9	35.2	15.4	39.4	15.7	41.2
Secondary individuals	2.4	3.0	2.3	2.2	2.4	1.9	1.2	1.3	0.9	0.9
Inmates of institutions	2.5	2.4	3.5	4.3	3.6	4.4	(NA)	(NA)	(NA)	(NA)
Labor force participation:										
Employed	30.9	9.9	26.8	10.2	26.2	10.0	21.1	7.8	19.0	8.0
Unemployed	1.7	0.4	1.3	0.4	1.0	0.3	1.2	0.4	1.4	0.5
Not in labor force	67.3	89.7	71.9	89.5	72.8	89.7	77.7	91.8	79.6	91.5
Living arrangements:										
Living in household	97.4	97.0	96.2	95.3	95.5	95.0	99.8	99.8	99.9	99.8
Living alone	(NA)	(NA)	13.1	28.6	14.1	33.8	14.8	38.0	14.9	40.3
Spouse present	73.2	36.9	67.9	34.1	69.9	33.9	77.3	37.6	76.5	36.7
Living with someone else	(NA)	(NA)	15.2	32.6	11.5	27.4	7.7	24.2	8.5	22.8
Not in household	2.6	3.0	3.8	4.7	4.5	5.0	0.2	0.2	0.1	0.2

SOURCE: *U.S. Bureau of the Census, Current Population Reports*, series P–23, nos. 57 and 59; series P–30, no. 306, and earlier reports, P–25, no. 643; and series P–20, nos. 105 and 106, 1977.

cent of women were employed in fields such as engineering, law, and medicine. The number of women managers and administrators increased about 22 percent from 1960 to 1970, but there were still about five times as many men as women in these positions in 1970. Earnings also show great disparity. For most groups, full-time year-round female workers earned 55–60 percent as much as men in 1974. The message is very clear: For the majority of Americans men are the career achievers. They occupy the breadwinner role in marriage—fulfilling, at best, a part-time role in the home. Women may have a career *and* a family, but the family is still the primary role. Women are hindered from greater fulfillment of their personhood by the inequality of professional career access. Men are discouraged from getting in touch with the full range of human emotions, thereby denying themselves the development of resources essential for fulfillment as a person. Women have learned to depend on men for major financial support, and men have learned to depend on women for affective support. This development of only half the person does not prepare individuals well for independence in the later years.

After 65, most men feel they have no means for expression of growth and continued development. Their training for life has been the breadwinning role. After 65 there is "no bread to win." Men have been taught from the very beginning to "be strong," that "big boys don't cry." The female, having been conditioned early to develop affective skills, appears to be more prepared to cope with independence in the later years. The primary role of the female during the young adult and middle years is nurturant and supportive. This role continues on into the later years for the female. The primary male role usually ceases at retirement. There has been continuity for the female role, but discontinuity for the male role. This sudden reversal presents a significant source of interpersonal problems for couples in the retirement years.

Although the role importance reversal may be difficult to cope with, we do not feel that it is debilitating or catastrophic. Individuals can change! With counseling, change is more likely to occur. (This process will be discussed in Chapters 4 and 5.) Young children today are beginning to be nurtured toward roles as more complete human beings. Male children are increasingly being allowed to cry, and females will increasingly be encouraged to pursue professional careers. As this happens, both will be more prepared to find satisfaction and fulfillment in the later years.

Marriage itself provides some elderly people with mechanisms for coping with situations that arise in old age. During the latter half of the life span married people tend to weather crises better. As age increases, married persons have fewer illnesses and lower suicide rates than the unmarried. Older married people tend to perceive themselves to be in better health and express more life satisfaction.

Marriage, or some type of couple relationship for the elderly, may be a major asset. *If* a couple remains in good health, their lives may be deeply enhanced by a close relationship. When one is ill, the other is there to provide nurturance. When one is lonely or depressed, the spouse has had years of experience dealing with this type of problem. For the happily married elderly couple, life may be rich in daily activity. Sexual relations may play a major role in marital satisfaction during the later years. Couples may find that even though frequency of intercourse declines, the sexual relationship takes on new and additional meanings that include companionship, being near the spouse, and more total sexual experiences involving touch, feeling, and high levels of emotion. Marital activity could include the formation of close friendships with other elderly couples as well as travel and extended freedom that has never been known before. If an elderly couple has an adequate financial background, life may indeed be at its best during the years following retirement. Independence may reach its peak, in that the demands of work and family have been removed by the years. These resources are important assets that can be used in the counseling process with older persons.

Unfortunately, for most this freedom does not continue. Fate intervenes, with the years bringing the earlier death of the male. The proportion of males over 65 who are married is about 79 percent, compared to about 40 percent for females. For those over 65, about 14 percent of men and about 50 percent of women are widowed.

Death of a spouse, death of close relatives and friends, illness, and poverty all appear to play a role in the decline of freedom and independent functioning. For many elderly people in these circumstances life is filled with despair. Life for older persons in this condition may be seen as horrible and too much to bear. Depression enters to a degree never before experienced, and feelings of hopelessness abound.

The later years should provide an opportunity for movement *to* life rather than *from* life. The last portion of the life span should provide satisfactions that were not possible during former years. Success throughout life is a *structured* thing. It is not built and maintained by fate, nor is it maintained in ignorance. Success is built from an awareness of factual occurrences and then a planned strategy to deal with these occurrences. Psychological intervention is a significant need for this stage of the life span.

RISING EDUCATIONAL LEVELS

As a twin effort, in conjunction with counseling, increased educational experiences offer the elderly additional resources for coping with the problems of later life. Preparation for old age should start very early in life, as young children are taught principles of independent living.

Professional training for the young woman should provide security throughout her life. If she should be required to support a household without the help of a spouse, professional competence will allow her to maintain dignity in addition to providing the necessities of life. Professional competence is but one small part of independent living. Competencies in dealing with other people and in being able to adapt and adjust to the necessity of moving to a new and different environment are necessary for both the male and the female.

Education in the United States has traditionally been the arena of youth. Adult education programs in many areas have tended to offer courses designed to increase employment opportunities. There is a trend in education now toward greater interest in the elderly. The concern is primarily a matter of economics. With a decline in birthrates university and community college programs will turn increasingly to that segment of the population that can make use of education and has time to develop it. This new effort to attract older persons will not only help overcome the adverse effects of sagging enrollments but it will enhance the resources of individuals in the later years. Cradle-to-grave modules will become common elements of educational outreach in the future. This offers a significant resource for use in building self-confidence essential to greater independence of the elderly.

The rising educational level of the young will promote the development of many resources that will be useful throughout the life span. The increasing emphasis on education will result in programs that will begin to reach more and more elderly. It can be expected that this rise in amount of education will only continue. The educational level of the average older person currently appears to be increasing at a very rapid rate. For example, those 55 and over who completed high school and college are growing in numbers. In 1950, 11 percent of the population over 55 had finished at least four years of high school. In 1970 the figure had jumped to 21 percent and to 27 percent in 1975. The proportion of older persons who had finished four years of college in 1950 was 4 percent. It had climbed to 7 percent in 1970 and 8 percent in 1975 (U.S. Bureau of the Census, Series P20, No. 295, 1976).

The increased educational level of the aged will have interesting consequences for the American society. If, indeed, educated people tend to be less complacent, then perhaps future generations of older Americans will be more aggressive in their drive to improve their frequently substandard level of living. Education tends to build higher expectations in a variety of areas (job satisfaction, income, location and characteristics of housing, etc.). As the numbers of highly educated elderly people increase, their power to see their expectations fulfilled within a democratic society will improve. It would be logical to assume that the more educated the elderly become, the more they will expect to maintain the standard of living they have grown accustomed to during the early years of their lives. This would presumably have the effect of maintaining their dignity as well.

At this time there are groups of educated elderly people who are increasingly willing to demand political action to lessen the problems that accompany age. The Philadelphia-based "Gray Panthers" and "Senior Power" are groups of this type. Future trends are going to reveal the development of additional groups of older persons who will become increasingly aggressive in pursuing their rights.

Many elderly have "educated" themselves, informally, to cope with life in ways that bring confidence, if not excitement, to the later years. Some have found that they can manage on their income quite well in areas where the cost of living is lower. Others have found creative cooperation among support groups of friends and relatives. Unfortunately, these support systems and lower-cost-of-living areas do not exist for every older individual. Increased emphasis on education for independence for all older persons is an essential investment, and one with high returns.

THE RISE OF THE YOUNG-OLD

If the population of the Americans between 55 and 75 years of age is examined, it can be seen to represent another age group all its own. Neugarten (1974) has described this group as the "young-old." At present they constitute approximately 15 percent of the population and will increase in numbers. They are generally more healthy, affluent, better educated, and more involved with life than ever before. More than 80 percent of the men and well over half of the women in this "young-old" group were married in 1970 and living with their spouses. Only 7 percent of the men and just over 30 percent of the women were widowed (Neugarten). Since increasing numbers of this group will be alive in their 80s and 90s, their potential for greater independent functioning would seem to play a large role in increasing optimistic and constructive views of aging. This emerging group suggests even greater diversity among the aging.

The increasing numbers of the older-elderly may result in more strained relations within this diverse age group. When social support systems are not present or are insufficiently supported, the accommodation of these elderly will rest more with the young-old (Neugarten). This has been seen in particular geographical locations that have experienced large migrations of the elderly over a short period of time.

SUMMARY

The context for psychological intervention must include an understanding of the way problems of aging have been faced in the past as well as an adequate description of current figures and trends of the elderly population. Historically, the early interest in the condition of aging focused on prevention. Aging was seen in a positive perspective, and the elderly were viewed as societal assets. After the Civil War aging came to be seen in more negative terms. The development of aging as a scientific area of study brought empirical results to support the abilities and potential of the aging. It is hoped that the increasing numbers of old people that eventually resulted in greater research interest will bring more significant political muscle to bear on their concerns, especially once their numbers become organized.

Concern is increasing for researching the actual independence potential available for development in the average older person. The enormity of this challenge is seen in the growing numbers of older Americans. Today, about 10.5 percent of the U.S. population is over 65. Greater diversity among the aging can be seen with the emergence of the "young-old." They will play an increasing role in changing society's negative perceptions of the elderly.

Chapter 2
Facts and Fables: The Physical Condition and Aging

The time has come when we need to move beyond the concept that individuals need no particular preparation for counseling old people. For example, an awareness of demographic data puts the whole subject of the elderly into a more clearly defined specialized area. A knowledge of basic parameters helps delineate this life stage with its own particularly unique needs from other stages. Our assumption is that any individual who expects to contribute positive and helpful counseling benefits to elderly persons must have at least a basic understanding of the aging process as well as a knowledge of the characteristics of persons in this developmental stage of life.

The physiological context of aging represents another area of understanding that is of importance to the counselor. Physiological functioning or dysfunction has been established as having a link to an individual's attitudes (Minuchin, 1974).

Society harbors a common myth that the physical *condition*, especially of the aged, is synonymous with physical *potential*. The elderly are particularly vulnerable to this myth because the effects of other general negative stereotypes have established a context for pessimism about aging. It is easier, under these circumstances, to believe that condition equals potential. Consequently, this evolving predisposition nurtures other associated psychological side effects. Lowered expectations reinforce doubts about continued contributions. Acceptance of a lack of potential results in loss of hope. Doubts about one's abilities coupled with increasing loss of hope bring significant likelihood of psychological dysfunction. It is important for the counselor to know a simple baseline of physiological decline in order to help the elderly cope with this myth, which can rob them of development of their residual potential.

Much of the popular discussion of physiology of aging is centered on the timeless search for avoiding growing old. From the very earliest times the challenge of prolonging the physical aging process has captured the imagination. These unfulfilled wishes were often found in the contemporary mythology. Aurora, a Greek goddess, requested immortality for her husband Tithonus, but realized, as he grew feeble and ravaged by age, her horrible mistake. She had forgotten to ask for accompanying eternal youth (Guillerme, 1963)! Alongside a concern for developing ways to take full advantage of old age the desire for eternal life was equally reflected in religious writings, literature, and even indirectly in the primitive medical prescriptions and potions, from ground-up animal testes to mixtures of plant tissue. Although the physical secrets of aging are elusive, they are closely tied to attitudes about aging and reasons for confidence during these years of the life cycle.

From centuries of experience we have gained sophistication, if not much success, in the search for unlimited life spans. However, much more is known about the aging process. Today the search for increased knowledge about physical aspects of aging has been primarily located in the areas of biology and physiology. Currently, many scientists have focused their attention on trying to break the secrets of DNA-RNA with hopes of some day discovering enough about how cells decline that a *reversal* of the aging process can be accomplished (Sinex, 1975). Although we have not solved the mystery of cellular aging, there is much that we do know about aging decline.

INDIVIDUAL DIFFERENCES

Fundamental to understanding the physical aspects of aging is the realization that although all individuals grow old, they do not do so in exactly the same way. Not only do individuals age at different rates, but different organs and subsystems within the individual age differently. Although the best data we have speak of decline in terms of general averages, these figures at the same time are quite misleading. To use "averages" the extremes at both ends of the continuum of decline must be included. Specific individuals will not age by the "average."

Biological aging is a universal, unidirectional, and multidimensional process. It is *universal* in that it happens to all living organisms. It is *unidirectional* in that there is only one way to go. A person cannot "grow young." It is *multidimensional* in that it occurs in many areas. Not only does the skin grow old, but hearing, vision, and many other areas are also involved in this unidirectional change that occurs with age.

Although great interest remains today in discovering the secrets for enabling people to escape the cycle of decline, the only conclusion that can be made is that it is inevitable. This process is seen in a number of biological subsystems. When decline is discussed, it must be remembered that we simply do not know the potential for development that the residual capacity itself holds. This is an extremely important element for counselors when dealing with older persons who use their declining physical condition as an excuse.

DECLINES IN RESERVE CAPACITY

The most obvious biological declines are seen in the dramatic drop in reserve capacity. All individuals have a physical reserve that is called upon in time of need. A weight lifter or professional athlete has a tremendous amount of reserve capacity to call into action when needed. Usually an older athlete will not be able to count on the same *amount* of reserve capacity that a young athlete will have. A paramount difference between the young and old athlete will be found in the amount of recovery time needed for the elderly person.

If, for example, a young person is winded by running up a flight of stairs, he or she will recover quickly. An old person may be able to run up the same flight of stairs, but much more time will be required for the aged individual to recover from the run. This decline in ability to return to prestress levels after reactions to physical (and even emotional) strain marks one of the most significant age-related developments. Responses of the level and intensity (physical and emotional) of earlier years decline. The aging person needs to allow more time to return to prestress levels. Again, the therapist must realize that although declines in reserve capacity are unidirectional, the potential for recovery will vary from individual to individual. *Condition is not synonymous with potential.*

CARDIOVASCULAR SYSTEM

There is little difference in the average rate of heartbeats in the normal younger and older adult *at rest.* The average is about 72 beats per minute. But, the difference is that, with the older person, the heart works harder to get the same amount of blood to the body. This reality leads to another development: increased blood pressure. Blood pressure is maintained by force of the cardiac contractions on the one hand and the resistance of the arteries on the other. Blood pressure is adjusted to meet demands made on the system. Diastolic and systolic blood pressure increases with age in most older persons. This will be more likely among older persons who have accumulated fat deposits around the heart and main arteries. The valves tend to become less pliable, and the arteries tend to narrow and become less elastic. More pressure is needed to push blood through the smaller openings. Permanently raised blood pressure can damage the arteries further. Low blood pressure, on the other hand, can cause temporary impairment of the blood supply to the brain, which may cause fainting. With increased age there is a tendency for clots to form inside damaged vessels. The most common problem in the later years is the loss of reserve capacities and the consequent inability for rapid response under stress. Cardiovascular diseases account for more fatalities in the United States than any other disease. They are so common from age 80 on that they were once thought to be synonymous with aging itself (Hendricks & Hendricks, 1977).

On the other hand, health care is constantly improving. The president's 1979 Biomedical Research Panel reported that human beings have within reach the capacity to control or prevent human disease. Earlier detection and better technology for treatment of such diseases as cancer, high blood pressure, kidney disease, heart disease, and mental illness will play a significant role in extending human potential throughout the life span (Kiplinger & Barach, 1979). The results are already visible. Although the United State hovers near the top among countries with high rates of heart disease, a 20 percent decline has occurred in the past 5 years. Great variability in rates exists. For example, in Japan the rate is 10 percent of that in the United States. Obviously, the condition of heart disease can be changed. *Condition is not synonymous with potential.*

RESPIRATORY SYSTEM

A general effect of aging experienced by most older persons is a reduction in respiratory efficiency. Older persons do not have the same cardiac output (pumping ability of the heart) as younger persons. As a result the vital capacity decreases generally, but this decrease varies from individual to individual. The average older individual will take in less air with each breath. Thus the expandability of the lungs decreases, so they contain smaller amounts of air upon maximum expansion; the residual volume after expiration is larger; the delivery of oxygen may be poorer because the oxygen has further to diffuse because of the fibrous material of the cells; and tissues cannot make use of the oxygen as effectively because of a decrease in metabolic rate. One of the reasons for decline in muscular capacity as early as the late 20s is due to decline in respiratory efficiency. Sustained muscular effort can be maintained for older men, however, if the effort does not approach the limits of performance and adequate rest pauses occur so as to avoid severe oxygen drains. *Condition is not synonymous with potential.*

THE SEXUAL SYSTEM

More emphasis will be given in this section to the sexual system for several reasons. The sexual functioning of older persons remains a taboo subject for most in our society. Many books on aging deal with the cardiovascular system, respiratory system, and so on, but few discuss the sexual system. Further, there are more emotional and attitudinal responses about sexual functioning than any other human system.

Coming to grips with the sexuality of the elderly from a frank and constructive point of view is a little like trying to play an honest card game with a stacked deck. Cultural forces work against efforts toward openness by reinforcing the attitude that elderly persons do not or should not need direct and continuing sexual satisfaction. If an older individual's sexual activity and interest are not voluntarily restrained, the *threat* of social criticism and ridicule looms as a major restrictive influence.

When sexual activity becomes restricted or eliminated through divorce or the death of a partner, an older person can become progressively disengaged and self-centered. The situation can lead to emotional problems (Levin, 1965). Continued sexual potency, however, helps prevent hostile, depressed, and lonely behavior patterns (Bowman, 1954). Many older men and women often refrain from continuing sexual activity or remarrying after the death or divorce of a spouse because even they have come to view sexual activity as a little ridiculous. The extent to which older persons have internalized society's concept of sexual activity being reserved for youth is demonstrated in a study by Cameron (1970). Among a sample of young (18–25), middle-aged (40–55), and elderly (65–79) individuals, the old judged themselves and were judged by others as being the least sexually knowledgeable, skillful, and desirous, possessing the least capacity and being provided the least access to partners.

A review of the literature of sexuality among older persons reveals several fairly consistent themes: actual sexual changes with age, frequency of sexual activity, attitudes and interest, antecedents and determinants of sexuality in the later years, and speculations on alternatives to marriage (Berezin, 1969). These themes will be discussed in detail in the next section.

SEX AND AGING

Aging females will find that certain physical changes have taken place since menopause: The breasts begin to sag; the vaginal lining becomes thinner; lubrication lessens and is delayed; the uterus decreases in size; the labial folds become thinner and smaller; the orgasmic phase is shortened; and loss of regularity of uterine spasms related to orgasm may occur.

For males the following major changes usually occur: Some tapering off of sexual interest may take place because of a decrease in the production of androgen; the testicles become less firm and smaller, and elevate less during intercourse; erections are somewhat less frequent; the prostate enlarges, probably due to reduction of amount of the male sex hormone; ejaculation may not occur with every coital experience; and erections are held for shorter durations (a 20-year-old, on the average, can hold an erection for one hour, whereas a 70-year-old male averages about 7 minutes). Physical changes in both males and females have been well documented by the Kinsey research and confirmed by subsequent studies.

There are no physiological reasons for elderly persons to stop sexual activity. Males may need more stimulation to hold erections longer, and females may need to make more use of synthetic lubrication, but neither is an adequate reason for the cessation of sexual intercourse.

The rates of sexual activity of older persons are fairly consistent among the major studies. The decline in frequency of sexual intercourse that is normally associated with the sixth decade and beyond has, in reality, begun to fall sharply by age 50 (Christensen & Gagon, 1965; Kimmel, 1974). Pfeiffer, Verwoerdt, and Davis (1974) found that the sharpest increase in the percentage of those admitting awareness of decline occurred in the age groups of 45–50 and 51–55.

The general conclusions about decline indicate that sexual interest and activity decrease in a stepwise manner with increasing age. The Duke longitudinal research found that two out of three men were sexually active in their 60s, two out of five in their 70s, and approximately one out of seven in their 80s. For women after 60, one out of five claimed to be sexually active (Pfeiffer, 1969). Other confirmations of continued sexual activity are reported by Amulree (1954), Christensen and Gagon (1965), Claman (1966), Finkle (1967), Finkle et al. (1959), Swartz (1966) Verwoerdt (1969), and Verwoerdt, Pfeiffer, and Wang (1967).

The frequency of intercourse for marrieds drops from an average of around 3.3 times weekly for couples in their teens to about once every 12 days at 60 years of age (Kinch, 1966). Kinsey found that females tend to overestimate the rate because they desire a lower frequency than males, while males tend to wish they were experiencing more than they actually are and thus underestimate.

Several studies of older single women revealed different results. Christensen and Johnson (1973) found 32 percent of never-marrieds had not experienced any sexual activity beyond simple petting, while 62 percent had experienced intercourse. By age 50, 25 percent were still involved in sexual intercourse (8 percent by age 60). Among single women who were divorced, separated, or widowed, 30 percent were having coitus at age 50, with the percentage dropping sharply by age 60 and to zero by age 65. The rates of masturbation for single older women were double that of married women (Christensen & Gagon, 1965).

The antecedents and determinants of continued sexuality in the later years include previous sexual experience, reasonable health, and the availability of a willing partner. Past experience seems to be an important determinant of present behavior, not only of frequency of intercourse but of sexual enjoyment as well. For women the enjoyment of sexual relations in younger years rather than the frequency is a more important determinant of present interest and frequency of intercourse. Marital status is a powerful determining factor in a woman's sexual behavior. For men, the more sexually active they were at younger ages the more active they will be in the later years (Pfeiffer & Davis, 1972, 1974). Benjamin (1958) found that extended sexual inactivity can be responsible for sexual weakness that is attributed falsely to aging. Alex Comfort (1976) warns against older men ceasing sexual activity for a long period of time. Secondary impotency may develop, making it difficult to begin again. Some of the more common causes of sexual dysfunction in aging males are: trying too hard; reactions to some drugs; some diseases like diabetes, hypothyroidism, multiple sclerosis, muscular dystrophy, stroke, and so on; psychological difficulties, such as depression, anxiety, phobias, performance fears, and the like; physical exhaustion; toxins; pain; infections; and obesity (Glover, 1977). Different drugs tend to suppress sexual interest. The physician prescribing the drug should be informed about any prescribed drug's effect on sexual interest. Often substitutes can be made which do not lower sexual interest. It appears that reasonable health, privacy, and having an available and willing partner are important factors for continued sexual intercourse. In those circumstances where the elderly are actually too infirm to engage in intercourse, the sexual needs of intimacy, closeness, and being held and touched continue.

Given these antecedents and determinants, there is no reason for the cessation of sexual activity in the later years. Much of the decline in sexual interest and activity among aging individuals is not physiological in origin. Pfeiffer (1969) reported that 86 percent of females who stopped intercourse did so because the husband had died, become ill, or had lost interest or potency. It is largely men who contribute to the lower level of sexual interest and activity of women. One remedy would seem to be in efforts directed at prolonging the vigor and independence and life span of men. Finkle (1973) found about 90 percent of male sexual impotency to be psychogenic in origin. Helping men to become aware of normal physical changes may relieve much anxiety about their sexual functioning.

For some individuals religious teachings are strong determinants for continued sexual activity in old age. Among the more strict religious traditions the purpose of sexuality is seen as reproduction. In the years following the reproductive period there is then no sanction for continued activity. For others the fear of inadequate performance, of a "turn-off" of the aging wrinkled body, and a mistaken interpretation of the failure to ejaculate at every coitus leads to decline in activity. These can be real problems for individuals, but they do not represent a condition of what has to be for aging individuals. Most of these psychogenic problems represent failures to come to grips with issues that have been present earlier in the life span.

Many people still have the sexual desire and ability for intercourse in the later years. There is evidence to indicate that sexual deprivation in old age may hinder longevity (Bowman, 1954; Kassel, 1974). To prevent feelings of loneliness, deprivation, and insecurity the aging person should have as active a sex life as possible. For patients in nursing homes Kassel (1966) reported the value of sexual orgasm for relieving anxiety as more desirable than the repeated use of tranquilizers.

How are the sexual needs of older individuals, especially women who have outlived their partners, to be satisfied? Victor Kassel (1966) argues for polygyny after 60, which he feels would offer the following: the excess numbers of women an opportunity to obtain a husband, the opportunity to reestablish a meaningful family group, more incentive to obtain an adequate diet, better living conditions through pooled funds, more persons to care for an individual experiencing illness, more sharing in household responsibilities, and a sexual partner.

Cavan (1973) suggests cohabitation or group marriage. Living together offers a reinstatement of husband and wife roles, a peer companion, and a sexual partner, all without legal and financial complications. Social pressure and the objections of their middle-aged children keep some elderly from this alternative (Bengston, 1975). Dean (1966) asked numbers of older couples in Miami, Florida, why they chose cohabitation. Their reasons included a strong need for security and companionship, as well as the fact that pooling resources enabled expenses to be met—with the disadvantages of legality outweighed by the benefits of expediency. Some older couples found the compulsion to secrecy and fear of possible scandal a problem. Others saw the companionship as the best therapy for growing old independently.

The capacity to function sexually into the later years is well established. The problem for many older persons is finding a partner in an acceptable relationship context. Extending the life span of males would help solve some of the felt sexual needs. But, until then, many older individuals who realize the value of continued sexual activity may have to choose between alternatives available.

AUDITORY SYSTEM

Hearing loss in the adult years is usually gradual and unnoticed. Most of the sounds that are important for an individual's behavior are well above the essential auditory level. Hearing loss, however, begins at a far younger age than most would imagine (Botwinick, 1973). Self-induced hearing declines often occur during the teenage years from voluntary or involuntary exposure to loud noises over a period of time. Very loud rock music, for example, can be detrimental to a person's hearing. With increasing age, changes will occur in reaction to frequency and intensity of sound (Atchley, 1977). Declines are considerable for high-pitched sounds but are small for low-pitched sounds (Bromley, 1966). These changes may explain why the low rich sounds of the organ are so very popular with the aged, whereas music with much higher notes is not so pleasant (Atchley, 1972). Atrophy of tissue, especially at the basal turn of the inner ear, probably results in the increased loss of higher tones. The very high tones are eventually lost completely. Stereo receivers with sophisticated equipment for delivering clear high tones will not be worth the money for the elderly.

Old people are also more susceptible to ear damage than young people (Atchley, 1977). Aged individuals should be cautious not to expose themselves to needless danger from very loud noises. Sounds emitted from industrial machines such as a jackhammer will damage the hearing of an older person much faster than that of a young person (Botwinick, 1973). Great caution should be used in protecting oneself from extreme noises such as a jet airline engine, or perhaps gunfire. Sex differences are also prevalent in hearing loss, with men experiencing much greater decline than women (Botwinick, 1973). For the older male, hearing loss is almost a certain reality that could and should be planned for. Looking ahead could allow planned compensation in the form of lip-reading practice and general practice in paying close attention to whoever is speaking. Some elderly people have gone one step further by learning sign language for the deaf in classes sponsored by senior citizen organizations. This ability to read sign language may allow a senior citizen group to participate in unique service projects as well as preparing themselves for the possibility of severe hearing decline at a future date.

VISUAL SYSTEM

As a person grows older, a number of distinct changes occur within the sensory systems responsible for the collection, organization, and distribution of data. An older person will experience a decline in the ability of the eyes to focus upon near objects (Atchley, 1972). Reading becomes more difficult, and corrective lenses may be required to compensate for declines in the ability to see things close up. One interesting aspect of this visual drop is that it does not affect all aspects of visual activity. Age does not appear to diminish significantly a person's ability to see distant objects.

With age the eye muscles weaken reducing capacity to change focus, to accommodate changes in the amounts of light entering the eyes (reducing reaction time to decreased light and glare), and to control convergence of lines of sight.

The eyes of an elderly person are able to admit approximately one-third the amount of light the eye of a younger person is able to admit (Atchley, 1977; Birren, 1964; Botwinik, 1973). This, of course, means that the elderly person needs more light in order to receive the same amount of visual stimulation a young person will receive. This is often more apparent in the work environment, where old people may be assumed to be incompetent because they are old, when in reality they may only need more light to see as well as the younger employee.

Night driving presents problems for the elderly that the young do not have to contend with. As the eye ages, it requires more time to adapt and recover from darkness (Botwinick, 1973). An old person driving at night will normally be blinded by the lights of an oncoming automobile more easily than a young person. In addition to being easily blinded, the elderly will require more time to recover from the temporary blindness caused by an approaching automobile. An awareness of these changes enables elderly persons to plan methods and strategies to compensate for decline in the eye's ability to adjust to darkness. For example, an older person who is aware of visual limitations may choose to limit the amount of nighttime driving as well as exerting additional effort toward caution.

The eye of the old person is less sensitive to color than the eye of the young as the lens gradually yellows and stiffens with age (Atchley, 1972). This decline means that more intense colors are required for the old person to obtain the same amount of visual stimulation that was received at a younger age. Therefore, it may be noted that older persons are often more attracted to more bright color combinations than they were when they were young. It also seems logical that more bright color combinations could be put to use in homes and long-term care facilities for the aged. Increased levels of visual stimulation could carry over into other areas such as motivation. Doors could be painted very bright, different colors in order to help persons locate their rooms. Elevator buttons may be different colors that correspond to the color of the wall that one immediately faces upon leaving the elevator. Having these colors different for each floor offers visual stimulation that helps orient the elderly residents. Throughout the spectrum of visual capabilities there is an age-related decline in sensitivity to light and ability to adjust to darkness, increasing farsightedness, and a general decline in ability to see different colors.

SKIN

As age increases, significant changes occur in the skin. The skin of an old person is less elastic than that of a young person. This decline can be demonstrated by pulling up the skin on the back of the hand of a young person and also an old person. If both the young and the old release the skin at the same time the old person's skin will decline much more slowly than the young person's. Men who work on shrimp boats and are exposed to sun, wind, and salt spray for many years find that their skin will begin to appear old and weatherbeaten at a relatively early age. Keeping the skin conditioned with artificial moisturizers and limiting the time spent in the sun and wind will help maintain its texture.

Biological aging of the skin is due, in part, to a substance that exists between the cells (as well as in many other places throughout the body). This extracellular substance, called *collagen*, hardens with age. The hardening causes the collagen to become more rigid, promoting the decline in elasticity of the skin. This decline in elasticity due to the build up of collagen is the reason the pinched skin of an older person will drop much more slowly that the pinched skin of a young person. This same process is involved in the formation of wrinkles. Although aging of the skin generally can be expected, the extent will vary with individuals.

BALANCE

One area that shows less decline during the middle years of life is that of balance (Atchley, 1972). Maximum sensitivity to balance will normally reach a peak somewhere between 40 and 50 years of age, whereas other senses tend to peak much earlier. Perhaps this helps explain the continued activity of some middle-age ballet dancers, trapeze artists, and other performers who have to rely on skill of balance. Beyond 60 years of age, however, there are obvious declines in abilities to reorient and maintain balance.

TASTE AND TOUCH CHANGES

The fact that taste acuity weakens with age has broad implications (Botwinick, 1973). For many persons eating is more than a necessity. The enjoyment of food may be a recreational activity that contributes a great deal toward one's satisfaction with life. As a person grows older, there is an increase in the amount of flavor needed to stimulate taste of certain types. The threshold of stimulation required in order for an elderly person to taste more highly seasoned foods increases a great deal after age 50. Therefore, a younger person who seasons food for the aged by taste alone may not satisfy the desires of the elderly person.

Sensitivity to touch is another area in which one may notice changes that occur with increasing age (Atchley, 1972; Botwinick, 1973). Touch acuity reaches a peak at around age 45 for most individuals (Botwinick, 1973) and then begins to decline. For example, not only does it take longer to pull away after touching a hot stove due to a general slowing of reflexes, but the perception of pain will actually be noticed at a slower rate than at a younger age. Other sense perceptions, such as hunger and thirst, may also be less intense than they were when the person was young. An old person may therefore allow more time to pass between meals. If a person is cooking for only himself or herself, time between meals may gradually expand so that a daily routine involving three meals decreases to a routine with only two meals, which may be further cut to only one. If the quality, as well as the quantity, of self-prepared foods decline, serious protein, vitamin, and mineral deficiencies can occur.

INTELLIGENCE CHANGES

Lack of knowledge concerning intelligence can lead a counselor to basic misinterpretation with the elderly. Evidence indicates that there are more differences among older persons with regard to intelligence than exist between older and younger generations. The expectation of an automatic decline in intelligence in all old people is a myth. Botwinick (1967) found the extent and rate of decline with age will vary from person to person, and from specific factor to factor under scrutiny.

Speed in problem solving and ability to solve novel problems declines somewhat. However, vocabulary could be better at age 70 than at age 30, since vocabulary ability is more a function of achievement than the ability to integrate (Botwinick, 1973). Memory seems to decline with age. Frankly, memory decline would not present a problem for prolonged independence for most elderly. Most positions of responsibility do not demand such a facile memory. Research evidence indicates that the individual's education is a more important predictor of continued mental ability than age. Further, Botwinick found that those who have more developed mental abilities at the beginning remain more capable in later life. The lack of emphasis on development among the aged is largely due to a feeling shared by many educators and therapists: that there is more potential in the development of younger persons. Much general support still exists for the myth, "you cannot teach an old dog new tricks." But there is little research evidence to support it. Data indicate that older persons may learn some functions a little slower, but they still learn quite effectively.

Response Patterns

Not only do old persons tend to move slower, but their capacity to judge speed and time declines (Atchley, 1972). Older people tend to underestimate speed, and consequently time appears to pass more quickly for the aged (Atchley, 1972; Birren, 1964). This underestimation of speed can be a problem in the driving habits of some old people.

In general, it is recognized among gerontologists that reaction time declines with age, but the degree varies among individuals. Why this decline occurs is not clear. One reason might be that older people seem to have a high desire for responding correctly. Drops in reaction times are based on test scores, which are usually timed. Older persons do not perform well on rigidly timed tests. However, if elderly subjects are presented with a complex task accompanied by generous time requirements, they do much better than young subjects.

Test Bias in Response Patterns

Lower scores by older persons on various tests and measuring devices need to be understood in context. Persons born during the same period of time (called cohorts) experience certain things that cause them to think differently from individuals not sharing these experiences. Cohort groups who have lived through the depression, for example, will score differently on certain types of psychological tests than those who have not experienced the depression. World War I cohorts may, as a group, think differently about serving their country than Vietnam cohorts. In other words, *experiences* may influence test scores even more than change that is due to age alone. Actually, age may account for very little differences, if it is not viewed with accompanying experiences.

Longitudinal versus cross-sectional collection of data is also very important in the assessment of the abilities of the elderly (Woodruff & Birren, 1975). The most accurate assessments of psychological abilities of the aged are conducted over an extended time period. In other words, a person may be tested when he or she is 20 years of age, then again at the age of 40, 60, 80, and so on. Unfortunately, this longitudinal method is usually impractical because of the time and costs involved. Most research with the elderly, by necessity, has focused upon cross-sectional data collection; that is, subjects of different ages are tested at the same time and the scores are compared. Many factors other than age may influence test results from cross-sectional data, such as cohort differences, socioeconomic status, educational background (including values, standard of living), and environmental influences (rural versus urban).

The *conditions* under which tests are given older persons are significantly related to their test results. For example, an elderly woman lay immobile in her nursing home bed for an eight-month period before the nursing staff realized that she could see fairly well if she wore glasses. She was not wearing the glasses when they brought her to the home and no one asked her if she wore glasses. She had been despondent, could not hear well, and was generally uncooperative. It was little wonder that she received unfavorable ratings with regard to testing potential. Dr. Charles Taylor (1977) described an intelligence test given to an elderly woman during which she was asked to name the president of the United States. "Why," she said, "Harry Truman" (he was president at the time). She took a piece of paper from her pocketbook, wrote down "Harry Truman" and put the paper in her coat pocket. The individual administering the test was curious and asked her why she did it. She said that she might be asked the same question again by someone and did not want to be embarrassed by not knowing the answer. This woman was very organized and efficient with her cognitive abilities. She was not only coping but was most creative in adjusting to potential future questions. Yet she could have been judged to be beyond help by test results. Many younger persons forget names when introduced, or write down names in a new group so they will remember them. The seriousness of forgetfulness in the old is usually given much more weight than in the young.

Factors that stimulate visual and auditory senses—such as the amount of light, the intensity of sound used in providing test instructions, the environment in which the test is given (i.e., home, office, lab, etc.)—as well as other factors such as the legibility of the test materials are of paramount importance in assessing the abilities of the elderly. For example, if written material is to be used with old people, the print should be as large as possible to allow easy reading of the material. The amount of practice a person has had in taking examinations will have a significant effect upon test scores. People with a higher level of education will do much better on most types of examinations than people with lower levels of education. Educated people are more likely to be *test wise.* They have usually had practice taking tests and are likely to be familiar with what is required for academically oriented achievement.

It could be that meaningfulness of the material causes score differences between groups of young and old subjects. Elderly people may not be as willing to tolerate the apparent irrelevance of many test situations that the young may find not only bearable but also amusing. The meaningfulness of the task appears to have far greater effect upon the aged than upon the young.

In many areas the active elderly are not only very proficient, but much more so than they were when they were young. If a person exerts even a reasonable amount of effort, cognitive abilities can remain strong and may peak very late in a person's life. Individuals who have been actively involved in intellectual pursuits and social activity most of their lives can and should maintain very active and alert minds. It appears that the human mind is affected by activity in much the same way that muscles are. Both require activity in order to maintain the capacity to function effectively. Programs offering intellectual, emotional, and psychological stimulation need not be reserved for the young and gifted. The beneficial effects of an enriched environment can aid immeasurably to the functioning capacity of the elderly even with cases of retardation and emotional disturbance.

Elderly people who are fortunate enough to be able to maintain an active life can expect to function in some areas as well or better in the later years as in earlier years. Not only do their total information skills increase, but noted increases are also found in vocabulary and comprehension. With age, a person who actively uses his or her vocabulary skills may expect these abilities to peak in old age. Comprehension and understanding also peak much later in life.

These results become clear when observation is made of highly productive, very capable elderly people. People who assume leadership positions—that is, bank presidents, government officials, corporation executives, and the like—are very seldom young people. The content of their intellectual capacity has required many years to build. What these people lack in physical and mental speed they more than make up in overall awareness and experience. Most executive decisions are made, not on a singular perspective, but upon a longitudinal assessment of many historical variables that serve to influence operation of the entire enterprise. The leader's job is to perform an overview of not one but many aspects of a company's performance. Perhaps this is the secret behind the glaring success of many old yet very powerful, effective, and dynamic leaders in high-level positions in government, industry, and labor. Leadership positions require abilities to view the entire situation, and to assess the potential overall effects of alternative decisions upon both long and short term goals and objectives. Compensation for the problems of age is gained from knowledge, awareness, and effective programs designed to enhance abilities to deal with often unpleasant realities.

It is important for the counselor to know what declines to expect with increased age and how they may be planned for. If a person is aware of probable areas of decline, steps may be taken to accept these and/or launch programs to avoid as much of the decline as possible. The authors are aware of one aged gerontologist who practiced writing with his left hand in order to prepare for a possible stroke that could paralyze his right arm.

The reality facing all humans is the universal occurrence of aging. Declines vary in rate from individual to individual, but eventually they will overtake each person. For centuries philosophers, medical doctors, and researchers have diligently searched for the secret of aging that will enable individuals to halt or even reverse the decline process.

COPING WITH DECLINE

Many of the physical problems (e.g., arthritis, osteoporosis, atherosclerosis, etc.) that become manifest in the later years are most ideally prepared for in early life. The earlier they are dealt with, the greater the probability of preventing or limiting their inhibiting effects. But the elderly can still do something. A systematic weight loss and physical exercise program can contribute significantly in terms of health, ability to perform physical activity, and prevention of skeletal failure (Lorenze, 1975). Too often the elderly are told what exercises they should not do. More encouragement is needed in terms of what they can and should be doing. In a study of men aged 52–88 exercise had the following results: increased the body's oxygen-carrying capacity; reduced body fat; reduced nervous tension; and improved heart and blood vessel function. Although DeVries emphasizes that exercise regimens should begin with caution, his program includes calisthenics, jogging, and swimming. The people who appear to cope with old age the best and live the longest seem to be the ones who intentionally keep themselves active during the later years (DeVries, 1973). In addition to exercise and diet, avoidance of tobacco and alcohol (the liver is less efficient in breaking down alcohol in the later years) has positive effects for keeping more fit in the aging years. State departments on aging are beginning to take leadership in projects designed to prolong independence. An example is Project Preventicare, which was initiated by a grant from the West Virginia Commission on Aging in 1970. Its concern is to develop physical fitness plans for older Americans. Physical fitness programs are sponsored for the elderly in senior centers, mental health centers, and personal care and nursing homes throughout the state. The program initiates such meetings as the International Conference on Gerokinesiatrics, which is the prevention and/or management of physical problems of the elderly by means of gymnastic or muscular action.

The goal of such exercise programs is not merely an extension of life but an improvement in the energy level and health of the elderly. These programs help contribute to that resource so important to quality of life for the elderly: the ability to affirm and celebrate life by never giving up.

SUMMARY

The potential for prolonged independence in the later years is related to the extent of actual physiological decline and activity level. Inasmuch as the best data we have on decline are presented in the form of "averages," the fact that individuals age at different rates makes it impossible to apply the *average* rates of decline to any one specific individual. However, eventual decline is inevitable. Average declines are seen in the lack of general capacity to return to prestress conditions. The cardiovascular system shows a vulnerability to lowered efficiency, but it is capable of continued development. Changes occur with age in the sexual system, but these developments are not sufficient reason to cease sexual functioning. With attention to reasonable rest pauses, the decline in the respiratory system can be managed by most older persons. Corrective medicine and technology help alleviate many problems of the auditory, visual, and endocrine systems. Test bias accounts for many inaccuracies in the ability of older persons. Basic information regarding physiological decline is essential for a therapist who works with the elderly. Not only is there a necessity to have this information, but even more important is the ability to interpret it.

What has unfortunately been communicated, indirectly, in the many exceptionally precise descriptions of aging decline is this: In American society the condition of aging has been taken to be synonymous with potential. Decline does not mean lack of potential. What we do not know is what proportion of the declining potential the older person is capable of developing for use in extending independence. An accurate description of aging could detail the process of decline to explain the *condition* of a 60-year-old who could not jog a mile. However, the description of decline cannot tell us what this 60-year-old's *potential* may be, given loss of excess weight and programmed exercise. The authors have followed, with interest, the San Francisco waiter who jogged ten miles daily in his later years until his death at age 107. The potential of older people is significant, but unfortunately the declines still receives the focus of attention in most texts on aging. Ruth Weg (1975) assures us, with respect to decline, that these changes are gradual and ". . . there is more than enough capacity left for independent living."

Chapter 3
Theoretical Beginnings

NEGATIVE STEREOTYPES OF THE AGING

There is a popular and pervasive folk wisdom in which it is claimed that "you cannot teach an old dog new tricks." Even many older persons subscribe to this belief. If individuals assume that they cannot learn well in the later years, a kind of self-fulfilling prophecy takes over. If this is the case, individuals who make the attempt to counsel older persons may find resistance. It does not take much unresponsiveness to discourage initiatives with this age group. For professionals there is little historical experience on which to draw. The old have, until relatively recent times, been the repository of accumulated wisdom. In this new period, change is so rapid as to have serious nullifying effects on accumulated knowledge. The old must be taught to adapt, but that is to be done without any traditions to inform and guide the teachers (Butler, 1975).

Resistance to endeavors at counseling the aged serves to confirm another facet of the popular wisdom about aging: that being cranky, uncooperative, and senile is inevitable for all old people (Butler, 1971). The lens through which society views aging consistently distorts the issue, and the result is highly negative and debilitating. The myths are additionally frustrating because there seems to be no way to cope with them effectively.

Evidence contradicting the negative stereotypes of the aging (de Beauvoir, 1972) is not a recent discovery. In the face of the evidence the myths persist. In most every conference and press release regarding the contemporary conditions surrounding the aged, some well-informed individual will pay his or her respects by condemning the negative stereotypes and calling for society to drop them from the cultural vocabulary. But the stereotypes and the exhortations persist. Articles are written condemning the negative characteristics of aging that have polarized around this segment of the life span, but, they continue with all their force. Books are written cataloging the insensitivities of society to its elderly patrons, but the insensitivities do not fade away once identified.

It seems few have noticed the ineffectiveness of the attempts to chase away these negative demons. But that does not seem quite fair. Surely it is apparent that as soon as the smoke clears, nothing has changed. What seems more likely is that there is a feeling of no options. Either one condemns the unhealthy atmosphere surrounding the aged or one is overwhelmed by it. The gnawing question of whether this approach has worked has not been addressed. If it were faced, the irony would be apparent: We have been diligent in scolding society for the stereotypes *and* have been overwhelmed by them at the same time. They seem to persist despite all our best efforts to dispel them.

Coping with the issue of negative stereotypes of aging is a central one for any counseling program. If the only therapeutic effort available is to continue to condemn the negative views of aging, the counseling effort will not get off the ground. Unless these views are dealt with, any therapeutic effort will continue to be undermined.

The time has come to take a new look at the negative stereotypes of aging. Since the stereotypes are so persistent, so resistant to efforts at eradication, they must be performing some useful function in society. If they have instructive functions with the elderly, it certainly is not apparent. But, with the young a different picture emerges. A society, for example, with high unemployment rates, particularly in younger age groups, will find little enthusiasm for efforts that tend to prolong economic and political control by the elderly. For the young, negative stereotypes are the leverage for changing the status quo control of the aging. To a large extent employment opportunities and promotions for the younger employees hinge on the retirement of older employees. Many employers have tended to feel that keeping the elderly on jobs longer deprives companies of the vitality, creativity, and zeal of younger employees. On the other hand, open criticism and direct calls for older employees to move out of status positions are not condoned by society. In this context negative stereotypes may help fulfill this larger societal need of the young. What appears to have happened is that the negative stereotypes of aging have become a type of "rite of passage" (culturally useful ceremonial for verification of transition from one stage of life to another). The now-amended retirement age (70) functions in this capacity as well. Many younger employment hopefuls enter the job market each year because of this age cutoff.

The negative stereotypes of aging contribute to the rite-of-passage transition of the older person, facilitating transfer of power and influence from the old to the young. This seems to be verified by the persistence of myths and negative stereotypes about the aged, in spite of ample evidence nullifying the negative characteristics.

If the persistence of negative stereotypes of aging is due to their contribution to the transition of power and opening of employment opportunities for younger generations, it will become apparent why they continue. Individuals who work with the elderly must recognize this function of the stereotypes. The negative attributions associated with aging have nothing to do with the actual potential of elderly persons. They serve as the most powerful indirect means available for economic and political power transition.

It is very important to see the distinction between the social use of stereotypes and the actual potential of older persons. As long as our society has unemployment problems, tight promotion tracks, and, last but not least, difficulty in tranferring power from old to young, we will have negative stereotypes. Silver-tongued oratory or highly praised literature will not stem this tide. *We had better accept this reality* if we want to counsel the elderly with effectiveness.

Negative stereotypes of aging will be with us in some form for the foreseeable future. This seems apparent. It also needs to become more apparent that they play a functional role in society and have no relationship to the actual potential of the elderly. One task and reason for therapy with the elderly is to help them see this very significant point. Internalizing this distinction is therapeutic in and of itself. It is the beginning of change. It is a freeing reality. Seen in this perspective, the stereotypes lose their power over individuals.

This puts aging in our culture in a new light. Rather than cursing ourselves and our aging destiny because of the stereotypes, they can become reminders for the elderly lest they drift into unnecessary personal decline. The stereotypes apparently function to obtain larger societal gains: employment opportunities, promotion options, and orderly transition of power. That elderly individuals take these negative characteristics of aging personally is a dreadful mistake. To do so is to fail to see their societal purpose. Properly understood, the negative stereotypes can be used constructively by the elderly. They can become reminders, cues for keeping the elderly individual more alert to taking responsibility for his own life. The process would work something like this:

NEGATIVE STEREOTYPE: All elderly are sick.

PURPOSE OF STEREOTYPE: To accumulate enough leverage to keep the *societal* transition of power from old to young maintained.

STEREOTYPE AS REMINDER: The stereotype serves only societal functions. It should remind me of that. Consequently, every negative stereotype I see can be a kind of cue for me to exercise my own potential and personal responsibility taking. This reminder reinforces the reality that what I do with my own life in these later years is up to me.

SENILITY IN CONTEXT

More than a decade ago Kastenbaum (1964) detailed the nature of problems facing therapists of the elderly. More recently these issues were raised in a different context (Garfinkel, 1975). In addition to the general problems from negative stereotyping, considerable difficulty seems to be based on the so-called "senility" condition of many elderly, which results in their apparent unwillingness to talk, to interact, in short to benefit from therapy.

Senility is commonly associated with aging and as such requires an effort to sort out the issues involved. The general characteristics that have been associated with senility include: confusional, hallucinatory, stuporous, comatose, delirious, and impaired recent memory, giving rise to illusional falsification, fleeting delusions, unsystematized, illogical, uncontrolled expression of emotions, and marked restlessness. Frances Carp (1969) has shown that senility may reflect cultural effects, medical illness, and personality variables. Carp relies on research that has shown senility to mask depression and anxiety. She obtained Senility Index scores from a group of 295 residentially independent elderly subjects with an average age of 72 (range: 52–92). Scores were also received from a group of 270 resident undergraduate students in a private liberal arts college in the same city. The average age was 20 (range: 17–25). Both groups had comparable IQ scores. Carp found that "senile signs" indicate maladjustment, neurosis, anxiety, or low ego strength. High scores on the Senility Index tended to be neurotic, dissatisfied, negativistic, socially inept, and unrealistic, and to hold unfavorable views of the self. There was no evidence that scores were associated with advanced age. The college students' scores were higher (more senile) than the scores of the old people. These results underscore the inappropriateness of identifying "senility" as age-specific. The characteristics may be apparent at all stages of the life cycle.

Senility represents a rather ill-defined term without physiological referrents and therefore has limited usefulness in counseling the elderly. Although cases of chronic and irreversible brain syndrome obviously exist among the elderly, symptoms usually associated with senility more than likely represent typical maladjustment problems.

The counselor must be aware of other ramifications that are involved in typical senility symptomatology. Subclinical malnutrition can result in the following characteristics: tired feelings, loss of energy, forgetfulness, not feeling like getting up or going out, headaches, and nausea. Ruth Weg (1976) described symptoms of confusion, hallucinations, apathy, and inability to concentrate and learn, as a result of vitamin, protein, and mineral deficiency. We also noted that institutionalized old persons with chronic brain syndrome (senility) were found to have vitamin B and C deficiency. Since stress tends to exhaust the supply of vitamin C in the body, the additional stress an older person lives through increases the need to get adequate nutrition.

GOALS OF PSYCHOLOGICAL INTERVENTION IN OLD AGE

Although the focus of the counseling process in this book is intended to be on elderly individuals with typical maladjustment problems, the approach is applicable to other age groups as well, especially individuals in the "preretirement" years. The strategies presented would have to be supplemented with the severe pathology of psychoses. Our efforts are directed toward the vast number of older persons who suffer from feelings of depression, diminished initiative, inadequacy, unrealistic goals, low self-concept, discouragement, and lack of sense of belonging.

More than 1000 Americans reach 65 years of age daily. There are, additionally, others in the preretirement years who will face many of the identical problems of those 65 and over. These older persons have arrived at this point, Elmore (1970) argues, because of or in spite of the following: early childhood experiences; attainment of goals and life satisfaction as an adult; presence or absence of physical or psychological disorder preceding aging; loss of important relations and friends; job and prestige; a supportive environment; and the disparaging attitude of Americans, including the aged, toward aging.

The elderly face a variety of problems for which counseling can be useful (Pressey and Pressey, 1972). Children leave home and start families of their own. Older parents often have difficulty with this transition. Friends die. Spouses become ill or die. Chronic illnesses develop. Retirement may bring serious psychological dislocation. Financial maintenance problems are typical. Roles and expectations are in transition. The general need of quality in life is present here as in other life-cycle stages. Bromley (1966) focused the irony of lack of attention to these counseling needs of elderly persons. He found it strange that so much of the efforts of the therapeutic community was devoted to childhood and adolescence when this period involves only one-fourth of our life span.

The process of adaptation, so important in older years, is not something new for the individual. Childhood experiences, choices made by the individual in response to his or her social environment represent important adaptation procedures that will be operative in old age. The directions personality takes in those early years will have its influence later in life. For example, an individual who learns, chooses, and is reinforced for those decisions that reflect more constructive independence will carry this resource into the later years. On the other hand, persons who learned early to channel their creative skills toward goals of manipulating others to serve them and to relieve them of the responsibilities life demands would be expected (in the absence of therapy) to continue these patterns in their later years. Maladaptive behavior exhibited by older persons is not understood by the present authors to be something new brought on by advancing years. Difficulties, open or camouflaged, that developed in childhood and were reinforced in adolescence, early adulthood, and middle age often present themselves in the aged. Whether the problems of aging are experienced as greater than those felt at the time of adolescence, or middle age for that matter, is open to question. But how the individual chooses to respond to the pressures, opportunities, and responsibilities of each age will normally take on a patterned style, which is not immediately apparent but is often detectable by the trained eye. The second half of the book will discuss these skills in more detail.

It is this *process* of growing old that must be studied, rather than the end product, Havighurst (1968) argued. The research on aging in the 1940s, for example, concentrated on the results of aging—declines, losses, and stresses—and showed very little interest in adjustment procedures. Over a 20-year period the aging process in a Kansas City sample was investigated. Havighurst's conclusions from these studies were that personality organization and coping style are the major factors in the life adjustment of the aging individual. The key concept is adaptation, an important process for dealing with changing life conditions. At all stages of the life cycle there are adaptation functions with respect to biological changes and changes in the social context. Life satisfaction would be a result of the adaptation process throughout the life cycle. Marriage, children, and career development are dealt with in early adulthood. In middle age the focus of adaptation is on career performance, family life, and civic involvement. During the age stage of 60–70 there are a number of potential areas with which the elderly individual must come to grips: loss of a spouse, energy and reserve capacity decline, loss of employment, and lowered expectations by others. From 70–80 maintenance of that newly restructured role for the 60–70 year period is foremost. Further losses usually occur, such as loss of spouse, family, and friends. Counseling services can offer a significant resource for enabling the elderly to develop the adaptation styles essential to life satisfaction.

The goals most appropriate for psychological intervention are not only adaptation to the aging process, but the circumvention of emotional and attitudinal problems that are likely to appear in preretirement years and later during retirement, including loss of vocational status and declining resources. A further goal is to fortify aging individuals with skills and abilities for celebrating life right up to the end. Most of the efforts to date have been with the first goal with an emphasis on cognition. There is a need for more balance, with greater attention being paid to the affective-emotional behaviors (Baltes, 1973).

Accumulating research evidence indicates the potential of older persons; for example, growing old can result in: a greater self-acceptance and increased feelings of satisfaction in life (Brown & Ritter, 1972; Coulter, 1968; Hickey, 1969; Reichard, Livson, & Peterson, 1962); increased experience and wisdom (Kleemier, 1961); intellectual functioning at least as well as when young (Schaie, 1975); and the ability to increase rational thinking and reduce and control anxiety (Keller, Brooking, & Croake, 1975). If Herbert Otto's (1966) estimate, that individuals operate at about 15 percent of their potential, is accepted, counselors can approach the challenge of increased freedom and independence for older persons with confidence, even in the face of the social reality of aging and the fact of physiological decline.

THE CONTEXT FOR INTERVENTION

Relative to resources available for the elderly prior to this decade, in recent years there has been a remarkable increase in services available for the elderly. Brody (1979) listed five service components common to both inpatient and community care. These services are designed to bridge the gap between independent living and the total-care facility: personal services, supportive medical services, personal care, maintenance, and counseling. Although this complete service coverage is not available in every locality, more urban areas are beginning to provide them.

Although the focus of this book is on a psychological systems model of intervention, it must be recognized that the contributions of the broader social system are essential. A counseling service pitched to the elderly cannot and will not work in a vacuum. Psychological support will have little impact on individuals with inadequate income, diet, health care, housing, and transportation. Consequently, an effective counseling approach will cooperate with and count on the support of social service systems that provide such resources as homemaker service, home health aid and assistance services, day centers, senior centers, employment services, nutritional programs, transportation, economic aid, and housing assistance programs.

With the increased proportion of elderly in the population the greater need for specialized services is being confronted by community-based counseling services. These centers are vital links in meeting the goals of psychological intervention with older persons. Prevention and enrichment, as well as adaptation strategies, are particularly applicable to this group. They may be reached prior to the onset of more severe maladaptive behavior.

As community-based centers become more specialized for treatment of the older population, the admissions to institutions will become increasingly characterized by the more severely maladapted and physically infirm. Nursing aides, attendants, staff, and nurses will need more training and support from the professional community for providing a therapeutic context. Even though only 5 percent of all the elderly reside in institutional settings, the concentration of maladaptive responses to aging presents enormous counseling needs. Because of the high probability of adaptation problems and the uniqueness of this group, new methods for intervention must be created.

More innovative models for counseling-service delivery must be developed that take into account the needs of the community and the special needs of the elderly (Patterson, 1976). Having a specialized service offers a referral source for all professionals in the community. Several model adult day treatment centers were established for this purpose (e.g., the Adult Day Treatment Center in Beverly Hills, California, and the Levindale Adult Treatment Center in Baltimore, Maryland). Specialized individual and group activity within a therapeutic environment is offered with a goal of reinvolving the patient in the community (Rathbone-McCuan & Levenson, 1975; Turbow, 1975).

BEGINNING COUNSELING APPROACHES WITH THE ELDERLY

Various isolated segments of theoretical approaches have appeared that offer perspectives for understanding the meaning of behavior in the midst of the process of aging. These developments represent a first step toward coming to grips with a larger theoretical model. These include the psychiatric approach, milieu therapy, reality orientation, behavior modification, and ecological intervention.

The most predominant avenue has been the psychiatric model, often referred to as the "medical model." The medical professional with the capacity to prescribe drug treatment is central. Although in the past the psychological resources have been largely psychoanalytic, in recent years they have expanded to include more varied approaches. A psychiatric approach has been used more with patients whose physical illnesses override social and emotional needs and individuals whose personality pathology is so severe as to find alleviation only through durg therapy.

Success from direct use of psychiatric intervention has been reported by Goldberg (1970). Forty patients over age 60 were referred to a psychiatric consultation team because of unmanageable behavior problems. Twenty-nine of the 30 patients given psychoactive medication showed enough improvement to allow staff to care for them in outpatient clinics. Conventional psychiatric techniques are not often used with the elderly because of lack of staff, lack of interest in the elderly, side effects of chemotherapy, and the condition of the patient (Chien, 1971). Therefore, Chien describes the success of wine and beer as substitutes for drug therapy. Drinking wine and beer allows for more social interaction, requires less medication, can reduce social anxiety, raises social participation, and provides some nutrition. Chien showed that with three groups of psychiatric patients the group drinking beer showed more improvement than the group taking prescribed drugs and drinking punch socially and the group taking prescribed drugs and not drinking either beer or punch socially.

England has experimented with a new approach to drug therapy with terminally ill elderly patients. Instead of ". . . lonely, drawn-out death hooked to tubes and machines on some hospital back ward or isolated nursing home room . . . a dignified, pain-free comfortable, easy death . . ." (Satchell, 1977, p. 23) is offered. This is brought about by offering a variety of techniques from predinner cocktails, recreation, day trips, and round-the-clock visits by relatives, young children, and pets to the use of heroin to control agonizing pain and anxiety. The hospital reports amazing positive responses by the patients, with a significant accomplishment—the ability to enjoy life right up to the end, even though terminally ill.

Milieu therapy (Cumming & Cumming, 1962) has emerged in the last 10 to 15 years and is growing in popularity. Its basic concerns are to change the drab, colorless, and mechanical surroundings of hospitals and nursing homes. For example, wards might be repainted, curtains hung, bedside cabinets provided for personal belongings, mirrors hung, pictures added to the walls, new furniture provided which affords an environment more in keeping with their residential living prior to being institutionalized (Cumming & Cumming, 1962; Gottsman, 1973; Heap et al., 1970; Sanders, Smith, & Weinman, 1967; Steer & Boger, 1975). Rules that required marching to dinner or an attendant present during a shower produce an environment that is foreign to the elderly.

A milieu treatment approach would change these and other autocratic rules with a view to providing as near a context as possible to the world the residents had become familiar with prior to the institutional admission. Even the attitudes of condescension and treatment of the aged as children would be discouraged in milieu treatment.

The milieu approach was designed for use with elderly in institutional settings. It has been assumed that it would be most beneficial to those residents who displayed listless and withdrawn patterns. It has been recently tested with the psychiatric-medically infirm (Steer & Boger, 1975).

Milieu therapy has reported significant success in promoting the resocialization of neuropsychiatric and geriatric patients as well as with the psychiatric-medically infirm (Cumming & Cumming, 1962; Heap et al., 1970; Sanders et al., 1967; Steer & Boger, 1975). Their results show that the more regressed a patient the more likely will he or she respond to the milieu approach.

Reality orientation therapy was created for older persons who experience a moderate to severe degree of memory loss, confusional states, and general disorientation. This approach is intended to be used early in the treatment process. Basically, in reality orientation therapy the older person is placed in groups that are intended to coerce him or her out of isolation and into moving back into a social context as a functioning contributor. This is accomplished in the groups through group pressures and interaction with other individuals. The patient is continually stimulated, intentionally, by repeated presentation of fundamental information, such as the day of the week, date, year, weather, next holiday, next meal (Barnes, 1974). It is assumed that keeping older persons active mentally is as crucial as keeping them alive physically.

Stephens (1969) reported successes with reality orientation in a four-year investigation. Barnes (1974) showed tendencies toward constructive success with reality orientation approaches, and seemed to feel that greater success would have been noted had the program lasted longer than the six-week period. Gubrium and Ksander (1975) raised some serious questions about the success of reality orientation in general and the situational transferability of therapeutic programs for institutionalized elders in particular. Citrin and Dixon (1977) found significant results with reality orientation procedures applied to confused and disoriented residents of an institution for the elderly.

The use of behavior modification with the elderly has increased recently (Baltes & Lascomb, 1975; Butler, 1971; Hoyer et al., 1974; McClannahan & Risley, 1975). A basic assumption of behavior modification procedures is that behavior is learned and therefore can be unlearned. Further, the elderly individual is not assumed to be incapable of responding physically and emotionally. The behaviorist simply assumes that behavior can be changed and proceeds to alter it to the extent possible. Behaviors to be changed are identified and defined so specifically that they can readily be measured or counted. The new, more desired behavior is defined equally specifically. It is assumed that if negative and positive reinforcers can be withdrawn, the unwanted behavior will extinguish, and if positive reinforcers are consistently applied to the new behavior, it will become more prominent.

With the use of behavior modification procedures a wide range of behaviors has been reported as successfully modified, such as exercise, verbal behavior, walking, social interaction, and screaming (Baltes & Lascomb, 1975; Hoyer et al., 1974; McDonald & Butler, 1974; Rebok & Hoyer, 1977; Simpson & Hoyer, 1974).

A very recent development for approaching the counseling needs of the aged is the ecological model (Baltes & Zerke, 1976). Deterioration in the aged person is seen as having its source in poor environmental conditions. Living in a deprived ecology is assumed to increase decline. This conceptual model assumes an interaction between unhealthy behavior patterns and the environment, which accelerates them. The intervention strategy that has been used in conjunction with this approach is behavior modification. Rebok and Hoyer (1977) use the ecological approach in combination with their behavior modification techniques. They argue that it is inappropriate to identify the individual or the situation as independent sources of the maladaptive behavior. Their position is that it is more productive to examine the interdependencies than to isolate one as the most important. One problem with this model is that not enough has been developed about the linkage between the older person, his or her behavior, and the social environment. This attempt at integration of a changing social environment and the aging individual's behavior and emotions offers significantly new directions for psychological intervention with the elderly. This ecological model is developed in Chapter 4 in detail.

The ecological model, which assumes a reciprocity of behavior and environment, has been supported by LeCompte and Williams (1970) and Wahler (1975). They reported high intercorrelations between certain settings and certain behaviors. Burgess, Clarke, and Hendee (1971) showed that environmental change produces behavior change. Baltes and Zerke (1976) reported success with teaching elderly nursing home residents to change dependency behavior and reacquire and maintain self-feeding skills.

All of these partial approaches to counseling the elderly have been useful and continue to be; see Table 3–1. The strength and weakness of all of these approaches are in their specificity. They are atomistic, focusing on parts of the whole, and thus are linear in orientation.

Table 3–1 BEGINNING COUNSELING APPROACHES WITH THE ELDERLY

Model	Stategies	Use	Strength	Weakness
Psychiatric	Chemotherapy, psychoanalysis	Physical illness, organic problems, behavior difficulties	Psychoactive drug therapy helpful in some cases	Not enough qualified staff; potential psychogenic source of "organic" symptoms; psychiatric treatment is usually very long
Milieu	Change physical environment of institution to one more like residential setting	Listless, withdrawn, and psychiatric-medically infirmed, generally more regressed patients	Promotes resocialization, improves general environment	Very general, not specific for one-to-one or one-to-family treatment; designed for use in institutional settings only
Reality	Continual stimulation by presentations of fundamental data, such as date, day of week, year, weather, next meal, next holiday	Memory loss, confusional states, general disorientation	Stimulates active mental processes	Designed for use in early treatment stages and for the disoriented

Behavior modification	Define undesirable and desirable behavior in behavioral terms; reinforce desired behavior, withdraw reinforcers from undesired behavior	All types of general behavioral problems	Easily learned; results usually are quick if the process is used correctly	Does not address itself to the social context that influences behaviors
Ecological	Same as with behavior modification plus examination of effect of social environment	All types of general behavioral dysfunction	Focus on specific behaviors and social context of behavior	Not enough known about linkages between individual behavior, and the social environment

THE LINEAR MODEL OF INTERVENTION

The linear model for counseling must be examined in more detail in order to understand the systems approach of this text. For decades the basic model for therapeutic intervention with individuals has followed the assumption that there are certain intrapsychic dynamics that are central to individual maladaptive behavior. The underlying proposition states that an individual's emotional and behavioral responses are to be understood and treated as isolated within the individual. Depression, for example, is explained in terms of psychological dynamics idiosyncratic to the individual. An elderly woman, 75 years of age, came for counseling with depression as the presenting problem. The symptoms had not persisted, and for long periods of time she was symptom-free, except for occasional relatively mild experiences. From a linear approach, the depression would be understood to be a kind of malfunction of the psychic system. Indeed, the middle-aged daughter described her mother's condition as a "sickness." Psychological intervention would concentrate, then, on sorting out and rearranging the psychic disturbance to reestablish inner health. If this did not work, drug prescription would be an alternative.

This approach has not been without its advocates, and its contributions in the field of psychological intervention cannot be overlooked. Serious problems with this model have been reported by many theorists and researchers (Baltes & Zerke, 1976; Rebok & Hoyer, 1977). Minuchin et al. (1975) see this linear model as too limiting because the problem behavior is seen as circumscribed within the individual. Diagnosis and treatment procedures focus on the individual. The result, with the depressed elderly woman, for example, is to see her social environment, healthy or unhealthy, as having no influence on her depressed condition. To a significant degree the linear model cuts the person off from the social environment for diagnosis and treatment and places all responsibility for change on the individual.

THE SYSTEMS MODEL

Research investigators and therapists have begun to focus on the influence of the stress-filled social situation in conjunction with individual personality typologies, the interaction of individuals in the social context and the feedback operations between the elderly individual and the social situation (Minuchin et al., 1975).

Elderly persons live within social contexts and experience interaction effects and feedback from their environment. They either live in a family with a mate present; in an extended family experience; residentially alone but within the social context of friends, of phone contact and visitation from family members, and of voluntary organizations; in an elderly residential living complex with varying degrees of health care; in nursing homes; or in various combinations of the above. What is characteristic of all of these arrangements is that the elderly live within a system including *the social context, interaction with that context,* and *operational feedback processes.* It is obvious that the elderly also live within even larger systems including legal, economic, transportation, education, communication, and service (public and private) components. These latter systems elements are of enormous importance to the issues of aging in the United States, but they are beyond the scope of this book. The focus here will be on the immediate social system of elderly individuals for the purpose of developing more appropriate psychological intervention strategies.

SOCIAL SYSTEM

A social system is meant to include the primary social situation within which the elderly person lives, moves, and principally relates. The emphasis is more on the interrelationships of a primary nature that are incorporated in daily social exchanges. Interaction is to whole persons rather than to role segments (clerk, salesperson, etc.) and includes more extensive communication with potential for personal satisfaction.

A couple relationship and the family represent examples of dynamic units within themselves. The events and experiences that affect one member will inevitably affect the other partner and all members of the family. For example, Helen, an elderly female, fell and broke her hip. The effects reverberated. Her husband, Bill, found his more or less independent schedule becoming severely curtailed. He had to care for Helen from morning to night with only a few breaks. Since he was not used to fixing meals, he had to check with Helen about every detail. He was a little more knowledgeable about cleaning the house. After two weeks he became increasingly depressed. One daughter, who lived in the same city, had been coming by after work to visit her mother every day. By the time she got home through all the traffic, supper for her own family was two hours late. The children were hungry and fussy. Her husband's usual pattern of supper, then time with the children, and finally two hours of office work before bed was in tatters. His usually well-prepared morning meetings with his office staff began to change. More irritation and tension began to develop in the office. His relationship with his wife began to show wear. The children's relationship with each other seemed more competitive for the parents' attention.

As Bill became more depressed, Helen began to lose some of the cheerfulness she had tried to maintain. In turn, Bill became less patient because Helen was less able to be appreciative of his contributions. The daughter became more involved and began cooking the supper meals during every afternoon visit after work. She began to complain to her sister, 100 miles away, pressing for some relief.

The dynamics of this family's social system, and others like it, are easily understood, and yet the usual psychological intervention strategies are offered under the premise that they do not exist. Psychological intervention at any point in the social system is usually formulated upon the linear model: The presenting problem is contained within the individual. If the daughter sought marriage counseling, the focus of her own individual personality typology and behavior would be too narrow. Her relationship with her husband as well as the social context of both generational families is the subject matter for marriage counseling.

If the father sought individual counseling, the therapist would severely limit the effectiveness of intervention if the depression were seen as a variable contained solely within the identified client. The entire social system must be examined. The therapist would want to know *what* is happening in the interaction between Bill and others within his social system. What are Bill's specific daily behavior patterns? What are the responses of others (feedback) to Bill's behavior? The system's approach assumes that behavior that affects one member affects all members. It is easy to see how Helen's fall has affected Bill. We can follow the behavior reverberations moving out like waves; Bill's behavior has shaped a response from his daughter, and so on. It is important at this point to plot the reverse movement: the process by which the response of the daughter (and others in the social system) shapes or affects the behavior of her father—in other words, feedback. The daughter's response (coming by after work *every* day and fixing the supper meal for both her mother and father) reinforced the father's depression. Had Bill's behavior been one of cheerful confidence at picking up the household chores, the daughter's response (feedback) would have, no doubt, been different. But it was her father's depressed behavior that signaled a protective response in the daughter that relieved father from the responsibility of cooking. Father received a reward for his depressed behavior. This basic reinforcement process will guarantee continued expressions of discouragement from him. The daughter's feedback affects father by reinforcing his depression. His return response of reinforced discouragement continues to affect the daughter.

Idiosyncratic personality typologies affect the response patterns, which can move the social system in completely different directions. For example, had Bill been a person who must busy himself with tasks to avoid threatening social interaction, different symptoms would have emerged. For this personality pattern getting involved in the care and protection of his wife could, subconsciously, permit him to avoid anxiety-producing situations. His wife would become his excuse. The symptoms exhibited by both Helen and Bill have meaning for the entire system. She may or may not have known that her symptoms would have kept him attentive and thus the cycle of response and feedback would have bound them together in a different way.

From this personality typology's effect on the system we could predict that if Helen's condition should improve, changes in Bill's behavior could be expected. If she became mobile and capable of handling old responsibilities, his excuse would have faded. He would more than likely develop a symptomatology to take the place of his social rationalization.

A stress-filled social situation in league with idiosyncratic personality typologies, interaction of the individuals in the social system, and the feedback processes constitutes a cenceptual model most appropriate for psychological intervention with the elderly.

The previous case of the 75-year-old woman's depression can now be understood and treated more effectively from this theoretical model. Her social context had been one of independence. Financially, she was able to make it from renting out rooms and from resources her husband had left her. The interaction with boarders had been a pleasant and rewarding experience for the most part. A new development had taken place in her social system. Her daughter's marriage had failed and she had come home to live with her mother. Gradually, the daughter took over more of the house, limiting the rooms available for rentals. She also began to assume more responsibility for household functions, buying furnishings, and changing the familiar patterns with only limited consultation with the mother. The daughter felt it would burden her mother too much and slow down her own desire to get the house in shape to take her mother into the decision-making process. It was about this time that the mother's depression became more difficult to manage. To have treated this older person's depression from the linear model alone—that is, as being contained within herself completely—would have resulted in predictable failure. To treat the depression as an isolated intrapsychic phenomenon and send the woman back into the social context that identifies her as "sick" would be of little therapeutic value. The social system would need examining. The daughter's interaction and mother's feedback reinforcement as well as the mother's interaction and daughter's feedback reinforcement are fundamental to dealing with the mother's depression.

This model calls for several basic changes in the counseling approach. Quite frequently a family will identify a specific member as *the problem.* All apparent *external* evidence seems to support this allegation. So in the typical situation the older person often is labeled as *the problem* and the therapist is expected to concentrate his efforts on curing the problem contained in the older person. In the systems approach the "labeled problem person" is not interpreted as the source of difficulty. This individual is seen as the "symptom bearer" of the immediate social system, which is understood as the problem. In other words, the family described above has no authentic "problem person." Bill might be seen as the symptom bearer, but the issue is a *family problem.* Consequently, the therapist would avoid singling out or reinforcing others' interpretations of any individual as *the problem.* Efforts at psychological intervention would be directed toward restructuring the response patterns of members of the social system. Special attention would be given to techniques for encouragement of responsibility taking, increased independence, and the development of an interactional context that encourages individual respect and cooperation.

If the workings of the social system are to be understood, the individual components and interaction processes must be examined. Basic patterns of personality are formulated early in the family.

INFLUENCES FROM THE FAMILY CONTEXT

The individual obtains the first and most basic information about what it means for him or her to be a social being from early experiences in the family. Family nurturance models and relationships among siblings have great influence on the individual in the first five years of life, and they are reinforced and extended during the entire life span. It is generally accepted among a number of family researchers that the basic personality, which will follow the individual throughout life, is formed by about age 5.

Cultural interests, intellectual goals, athletics, family cooperation, or religious involvement are usually set in motion for the individual according to the extent that they are valued by the family. The interests, or lack thereof, that the older person displays will be understood better by a close examination of the original family context. The personalities of older individuals, even from the same family, will usually be quite different from each other. The unique characteristics of each individual are to a large extent influenced by the individual's sibling position in his or her orginal family and the accompanying competitive quality of most families.

Each old person had a distinct position in his or her original family. This particular position will influence the person's understanding of life and self-understanding as much in the later years as in earlier years. The positions to be considered are: oldest, second, middle, youngest, and only. Alfred Adler (1929, 1931) was one of the first to documents this early development, and others later expanded it (Ansbacher & Ansbacher, 1956; Toman, 1976).

The traditional characteristics of these sibling positions are understood to be nomothetic in nature; that is, they are general characteristics, but they may not be generalizable to all situations. The oldest child usually shows more interest in order, structure, authority, conformity, and generally dislikes change (it was change that brought the original disruption by the entrance of the second born); may be more conservative; more likely to attend college; and later is more likely to be found in positions of management and supervision. This is a natural outgrowth from parents' tendency to give responsibility to the oldest child, who at the time seems most able to handle it. Oldest children grow up usually feeling quite comfortable with handling responsibility.

The second child normally has spent all his or her days in the presence of an older, larger, more capable sibling. (Exceptions to this include the case when the first child is handicapped.) The second child tends to see the oldest child as the "pacemaker." At first the second may feel inferior to the first. The second will then compete and try to overtake and supplant the first child's position of attention and affection. If there is much competition, the second child usually seeks his or her place in the family by becoming the opposite of the first, giving over to the first child the areas in which there do not seem to be possibilities for success.

The second child will frequently be more of a rebel, more creative, more open to and desirous for change than the first child and may see change as the means of gaining the advantage over the first. Consequently, the second child is less consistent in carrying out ideas than the first.

If there is a third child, the second will feel displaced at both ends. He or she must compete with the oldest child (larger, stronger, and more capable usually) and has to compete with the third child for the parents' attention and affection. This leads to frequent vacillation between the desire to be responsible like the oldest child or to be a baby like the youngest. If unable to cope with this situation successfully, the middle child often becomes overconcerned with injustices, often complaining outwardly or seething within over alleged unfair treatment. This approach gives a new perspective to the conformity and responsibility of one elderly person and the puzzling protests of continual inequities from another.

The youngest child has a kind of unique advantage. He or she is never displaced. The larger the family the more enviable is this position. There are a host of budding "mommas" and "daddies" eager to either gain parental approval by babying this child or gaining some leverage with parents by pointing out his or her inadequacies and special privileges. The youngest seldom gets taken seriously by his or her siblings. But they respond favorably when the youngest makes some cute remark, is charming, or appears the most helpless.

The youngest child is likely to take one of two directions: either to channel his or her energies and abilities to press others into service or to become so competitive that the consuming goal will be to outdo, to outshine all of the siblings. Whichever route is taken, he or she is likely to feel loved when at the center of attention and when others see to his or her basic needs. The youngest child often attains the center by being funny, dramatic, helpless, or so good at something that others take notice. Youngest children are capable of handling responsibility well, *if they choose it.*

The only child has many of the characteristics of the oldest child, with a few additions. In reality, the only child has no sibling position and is never displaced. The only child lives primarily in the company of adults, is core oriented toward older individuals, and has a little more difficult time getting along with peers. He or she knows better than other children how to handle adults, how to involve them for his or her own purposes. Outside the family this child wants to be in the limelight, under the guidance and protection of older people, or persons in authority positions.

Knowing the family context and "perceived" sibling order will give older individuals and professionals significant information that can help make sense of normally puzzling behavior. Much usefulness exists for "perceived" sibling order information of older individuals for understanding the directions the social system will take due to the individual interaction and feedback. Murray Bowen (1978) describes sibling order information as the most valuable single bit of information for understanding a system's interaction process.

> Virginia, a 68-year-old living with her husband, wanted to participate in several local clubs to which she had been invited. She complained to her husband that she was not smart enough to feel comfortable with those ladies who were always coming up with ideas for helping the community which she felt were too complicated for her. Her husband had been puzzled by this behavior for years and had felt sorry for her by protecting her from challenging social situations. She would reveal in a casual conversation quite creative insight and ideas, but deny confidence in herself in a group of women. On occasion, her husband would lose patience with her and ridicule her inadequacy feelings. This upset her and the upsetness was additional reason for being unable to socially interact. Her sibling position revealed helpful information for a system intervention. She had an older sister who was not very outgoing but who received her parents' praise for exceptionally good grades. Virginia decided early she could not compete with her sister for recognition from grades but did receive much parental and extrafamilial response for her

friendliness. She chose to emphasize other areas for praise from her parents but made the mistake of concluding that she was not very smart. Actually Virginia's choice not to develop, significantly, her intellectual skills had nothing to do with her actual ability. Her husband's feedback reinforced the excuse for avoiding social responsibility. This new level of insight gave her more confidence to begin to develop her intellectual skills which had laid dormant for all these years. A systems interpretation enabled the husband to change his feedback interaction. She felt better about herself after she saw how she had come to lack confidence in her intellectual abilities.

Thus sibling information can offer clues about why the response configurations in a social system take certain specific directions. Patterns of behavior that developed early in families continue into old age. Although sibling order is useful in determining how certain types of behavior began, we need to know more if we are to interpret the way these early patterns have been integrated and how they motivate current behavior.

BEHAVIOR IS PURPOSIVE

The fact that some elderly individuals see events and circumstances in a positive way and others see them quite pessimistically suggests certain underlying assumptions about the meaning or purpose of this behavior in response to these life situations. There seems to be evidence to support the conclusion that it is not events that possess power over us. Rather, it is we who bestow power on events. We interpret circumstances either as too much for us to handle or as situations that, with courage, we can handle (Ansbacher & Ansbacher, 1956; Mosak & Dreikurs, 1973). If individuals really do have the final freedom of choosing how they will respond to circumstances in their life (Frankl, 1963) it will be helpful to decipher the meaning or purpose of behavior of older persons.

A different and very productive approach for understanding the behavior of older persons is emerging (Mosak & Dreikurs, 1973; Nikelly, 1971). The assumption is that behavior has a goal (or goals); it has an intention that usually is not apparent to the individual. The goal can be conceived in terms of a "payoff," reinforcement, secondary gain. The process involved is one of "analyzing the goal" of the behavior.

In this approach "present" behavior is critical. This action is always seen as taking place in a social system. Behavior in the past is not considered unimportant but is informative mainly to the extent that it may illuminate present behavior. An increasing number of professionals have responsibilities that make it very critical that they understand the meaning of the behavior of older persons. Making use of the concept of "purpose" of behavior can be a great asset for these persons. When confronted by puzzling or contradictory behavior we ask ourselves: "What is the (present) goal of this behavior? What is the (present) payoff to the older person? What are the secondary gains? To increase the likelihood of understanding the individual's "goal" we ask the person: *What happens when this behavior is manifested? What do persons around the individual in question tend to feel, say, and do?* These questions should be pressed for specific details. (Case study examples are presented in Chapter 6.)

Mr. Biggs, an active elderly male, 71, registered for courses offered by the local college. When the subject of age came up Mr. Biggs, in a forceful and knowledgeable manner, would suggest to the class that all of this "theory stuff" was OK for the ivory tower, but that it would not work in the real world. "If you want to know where the truth really is," he suggested, "then you should get out of your ivory tower and live in the real world of aging individuals." Mr. Biggs was also a regular member of a local American Association of Retired Persons chapter. He never missed an opportunity at the weekly meetings to tell the group of fellow retirees how unrealistic and rigid they were not to take advantage of continuing education. "If you have any idea of what is good for you," he insisted, "you will enroll at the college and take advantage of opportunities to keep up on the latest knowledge."

How does one make sense of this contradictory behavior? Again, let's ask the key question, how do people in his social system respond? By isolating the "payoff," the goal, we will have understood more accurately what is going on. At the class, the feedback from class members reinforces Mr. Biggs's behavior. They are impressed with the forthrightness and apparent confidence of Mr. Biggs. "Perhaps he is right," some would say. "After all, he knows what it is really like." In the class Mr. Biggs gained a favored position over other class members by not having to be responsible for anything. In the eyes of some students he lifts himself above the instructor without having to learn, produce, or contribute anything.

At the local chapter meeting, many individuals, though perhaps not liking Mr. Biggs's style, nevertheless were impressed by the fact that he was involved in grappling with new ideas and keeping up on new knowledge. At the group meeting, where Mr. Biggs contended the "real world" existed, he deliberately set himself up in a favored position.

By pursuing our original question of how people in the social system respond to a particular behavior, we have discovered a common goal. The puzzling unexplainable behavior becomes clear. Mr. Biggs's "purpose" is to feel comfortable, to feel he belongs, by setting up situations where he is in *control* without having to be a responsible student or AARP member. He takes control of the class by ridiculing education; he controls the local chapter of the American Association of Retired Persons by exalting education. He attains a favored position without having to "do" anything.

Orienting yourself toward looking for the "goal" of behavior is to be distinguished from the more popular approach of looking for the "cause(s)" of behavior. Since this approach can also be used with residents in nursing homes, the following case study reflects this context.

Martha, a 73-year-old female guest in a modern, well-equipped nursing home, refuses to participate in the exercise program. She usually makes a big fuss about it. She has no health problems or physical hindrances; she just continually refuses to cooperate. If you were looking for the "cause" of the behavior you might conclude: (1) Perhaps Martha does not feel confident; (2) she may not feel comfortable because of previous experiences of failure at exercising; (3) Martha may be a very shy person, and this keeps her from participating; (4) Martha may not have had parents and teachers who helped her feel confident about herself. The list could go on and on. There are difficulties with seeking "causes" of behavior. Each "cause" has been affected not only by a previous "cause" but by combinations of "causes." A second problem about "causes" is that once you have identified a "cause," a potential source for "blaming" has been established. Blaming is a common pattern for avoiding social responsibility. A principal goal of healthy relating involves the individual assuming responsibility for his or her own behavior. Identifying a "cause" often provides the individual with a convenient excuse for avoiding responsibility for his or her behavior.

To find the "purpose" of Martha's behavior in her social system we might first ask, "What happens when she makes a fuss about not exercising? How do persons around her respond? The recreation director tries very hard to convince Martha that exercise will be good for her, that joining the group will make her feel better. After this daily routine at exercise time the recreation leader finally has to leave Martha in order not to be any later than she already is for the group exercises. Each day, as soon as the recreation leader departs, a student volunteer, who feels sorry for Martha, comes to sit with her until the group exercise is over. What is the meaning of the daily refusal to participate in the exercise program? The "payoff" is more clear in this case. Martha has attained 15 minutes of the recreation director's time daily, and in spite of the demands on the volunteer from the other residents, Martha has the undivided attention of the volunteer for the duration of the exercise program and often for a longer period.

Under these circumstances we would see no reason for Martha to change her behavior. She is getting too much "payoff" for her behavior through the feedback of the recreation director and student. It may not be the most positive situation, but arguing with the recreation director is better than being ignored. Unconsciously, the feedback from the recreation director and the volunteer is encouraging Martha's lack of cooperation. Positive benefits of group involvement and exercise are lost.

RECURRING PATTERNS OF UNPRODUCTIVE BEHAVIOR IN SYSTEM INTERACTION

It is always easier to understand the meaning of a behavior that is discussed with a case study in a book than to understand the meaning of a particular behavior in a real-life situation. What is needed is a guide that will provide direction for the practitioner in most situations that will be confronted. This kind of interpretive tool is essential if it is necessary to modify the behavior of the older person.

There are some common patterns of behavior in social systems that can be identified. These have been summarized in the characterization of the ABCs of unproductive behavior that follows (Allred, 1968). This model offers the practitioner a down-to-earth description of the psychological motivation of the older person. It offers a useful process that will be readily applicable to behavior patterns of the elderly who are fairly independent as well as those who are institutionalized.

Those who work with the elderly may have difficulty believing that older persons' unproductive behavior in social systems can be characterized by one or other of the levels of behavior listed. Some will object on the grounds that any attempt to organize levels of behavior among older persons is too simplistic. We would encourage the reader to raise objections about the model and, quite simply, not to accept it at face value. If it seems to fit in your counseling intervention with older persons, then it can be useful. It may not work for you. This approach represents an attempt at further defining "handles" for counseling older persons and, as such, must be able to stand the test of research and clinical use. This discussion will focus on the description of the levels of unproductive behavior. A later chapter will include techniques for identifying and applying these various levels.

Level one of the ABCs of unproductive behavior we have labeled as "Attention gaining." The second level is characterized as an attempt to be "Bossy," and thereby establish his power. Level three, which we call "Counter-hurt," implies the only way the individual feels worthwhile is to carry out revenge on others whom he feels have hurt him. Level four is described as "Disablement," which involves the portrayal of deficiencies in order to be left alone. These four "levels" characterize the typical patterns of unproductive behavior in older persons.

The older person may be at several levels at the same time, or with different people may display a different level. Usually, however, there will be one level that is more predominant. No matter what level the individual may be operating from, it is the meaning of the behavior that is more important. The assumption is that only by behaving in the level demonstrated will he or she be significant. The individual at any given level will utilize a variety of methods, from time to time, to secure a goal.

The behavior at these various levels may be directed toward their own children, their spouses, and their peers. A fake and fleeting sense of worth and significance seems better than nothing and can be achieved more easily through unproductive behavior levels than an authentic sense of belonging and value from independence and individual achievement. This reality serves to reinforce the four levels of unproductive behavior.

Level one, "Attention gaining," is found in most elderly individuals. It is especially characteristic of this society that few outlets for productive behavior are recognized for the aging. Therefore, fewer constructive outlets are available for elderly than for other age groupings for establishing a sense of "social belonging" and accomplishment. Their children are usually busy with their own families, needs, and social development. Little time is available for the older parents. For most, retirement has taken away any opportunity for accomplishment and status through vocational activity. Recipients of the thousands of cues of expected inadequacy, the elderly often move toward seeking affirmation of their acceptance through what attention they can squeeze from others. Since this unproductive behavior does not really satisfy the inner needs for preservation of independence and belief in one's own capacities, the individual seeks even more repetitively new evidence that will show that he or she is not useless and alone.

All attention seeking is not unproductive. Every individual finds attention useful. The distinction between healthy attention getting and unproductive attention getting is *reciprocity*. Giving and receiving attention, a reciprocal relationship, represent healthy behavior. Behavior oriented primarily around only *getting* attention is usually characterized by unproductive mechanisms.

As those who are the objects of his attention-gaining behavior get increasingly annoyed, the older person may push harder with these attention-gaining techniques. This feedback usually serves to push others further away. Reactions usually take the form of further distance or attempts to talk the older individual out of his other attention-gaining behavior. Trying to talk the older person out of the behavior serves his or her purpose: The individual has gained the center of attention, and the systemic circle of action-feedback is complete.

If the older person's "attention gaining" increases social distance from the person in mind, or if others try to stifle attention-gaining moves, the individual tends to move to level two, "Bossy" behavior. Those who relate to the older person may try to stop the annoying behavior patterns by asserting more control. Since the one in control represents power (and unfortunately, worth), a struggle is inevitable. The older person, especially if he or she was a parent, has a special feeling about who should be in charge. This has been his role and source of status for decades. The struggle for power continues between parent and child. Those who work professionally with older people are often special targets of rebellion for level-two individuals, especially if they are young. They are often seen as symbols of their children, with whom they can relate only when it has been clearly established who is boss.

In family settings, the elderly often demonstrate their bossy behavior through efforts to control the grandchildren or the spouse. Interference with discipline of the grandchildren can be an open display of who is boss. Grandparents may use grandchildren as pawns by establishing a never-ending flow of presents in an effort to gain an upper hand in the power struggle with their own child.

With the older person in an institutional setting, bossy (or controlling) behavior is often demonstrated by refusing to cooperate, follow rules, or comply with simple personal hygiene. Interpreted, this behavior means: You think you can control my life. I will show you who is boss. You cannot make me follow your rules.

Once a power struggle has been established the relationship between the older individual and the other person(s) in the conflict usually deteriorates. Hurts usually result and the older person may move to the next level, "Counter-hurt."

Level three or unproductive behavior involves older persons who feel deeply rejected. They feel they cannot obtain any significance by attention gaining or by bossing the people in their social environment. The hurt that has resulted from the power struggle with others is too great, the behavior pattern much too established to break out into any other emotional response pattern. The logical extension behaviorally, is level three, "Counter-hurt." The old person feels hurt and now is so discouraged that he seeks his place by being revengeful. A rather consistent role pattern unfolds: every relationship is examined not for its giving and sharing potential, but to pick out clues of intended or imagined hurts. The older person at this level cherishes mutual antagonism and actually feels a satisfaction when he or she succeeds in hurting others. It is as if there is a kind of symbolic trophy to be obtained every time there appears to be justification for being cruel. For the individual to feel justified in remaining cruel, continued provocation is necessary. To assure a continuing supply of evidence that others have hurt them, these individuals find themselves caught up in a systems process of action-feedback-action in which they, subconsciously, evoke from others in their environment the type of behavior which then seems to justify their desire to counter-hurt.

Level three can so intensify between the older person and others in his or her life that severe discouragement sets in. This represents the fourth and most severe level of unproductive behavior. Faith in his potential is gone and the person seeks to avoid any expectation from others that he or she will be productive and cooperative. The passive qualities that began as efforts to gain attention and a favored position have now reached their extreme conclusion: Such people are so convinced of their inadequacy that they do not attempt to take responsibility any more. Their actions are very clear: *Leave me alone.* However, a delicate balance is sought. The desire to be left alone is not absolute. These people's desire is to be left alone with respect to any demand or expectation. By avoiding responsibility, the feeling is that further experiences of failure will not occur.

These levels of behavior may appear more complex than they actually are. In actuality, any practitioner can learn how to interpret the purpose of unproductive behavior by carefully examining what happens in the transactions and what payoff is received from feedback within the system. This should be done with supervision from trained therapists. Techniques for dealing with these levels of behavior are presented in Chapter 5.

Let us bring this new approach back to our earlier discussion of the paradoxical situation regarding older persons in general. We pointed out the evidence for continued growth and development throughout the life span. In spite of society's stereotypes, many older persons choose to face life with courage. We also discussed the heavy negative stereotyping of age often assumed by the elderly themselves. Why do many other older persons often not only assume that they are supposed to be cranky, uncooperative, and irritable but feel compelled to act out this role? How can we make sense of this contradictory behavior? By becoming more aware of how people around older persons respond to their behavior we get clues as to its meaning. Too often, courageous positive behavior is taken for granted. How do people around the elderly respond to cranky, irritable, and uncooperative individuals? Usually by giving feedback in large amounts of attention trying to convince them that there are reasons for being happy and benefits to being cooperative, or giving attention under the assumption that a lot of attention will encourage more mellowness. Occasionally the professional's behavior communicates exasperation and a giving up on expecting anything of the older individual. There is then little external payoff for continuing to face life courageously. This reinforced feedback becomes useful to the individual for avoiding responsible behavior. Cooperative, responsible behavior so often gets ignored. But, how can you *guarantee* that people will pay attention to you? By being cranky, uncooperative, and irritable! It has negative side effects, but it seems better than being ignored. The old saying, "It is the squeaking wheel that gets oiled," is alive and well!

We forget that older persons can be as clever as adolescents at turning life's apparent disadvantages into styles for coping with their world. It is like taking the "lemons" life seems to have dealt them (negative stereotypes) and now turning them into lemonade. This involves a lot of creativity and is further evidence of the enormous potential of older persons. The rationale goes something like this: If society views the elderly in negative ways, the older person can use this as a handy source of blame for his or her problems. (It is becoming more apparent that blame is at the bottom of most neuroses; see Ellis & Harper, 1976.) Further payoff is to be found if the individual is cranky, uncooperative and irritable: People will pay attention *and* little will be expected in return, except that he or she be cranky, irritable, and uncooperative. Responsibility for one's own life and for others can be avoided without feeling too many pangs of conscience: *That's the way society expects me to be.* Society's stereotypes can be used to avoid responsibility within the elderly individual's social system.

If this is true, or to the extent that it is true, we can conclude that the older person is not totally the victim of society's stereotypes, but may in fact actively influence the stereotyping. Without being consciously aware of it, many elderly persons know how to gain an advantage from society's rejection of aging.

A strong case can be made for events having no power in themselves. Events, occurrences in one's life, can be seen as catastrophic, formidable, or manageable by the interpretation we give to them. If a person *believes* a rattlesnake is in the next room, even if it is not true, no amount of convincing will alleviate the fear. If an individual believes it is tragic to grow old, then growing old will be a tragic experience. If a person believes growing old is an experience of continued growth and development, growth and development will continue (given reasonable health). It is beginning to be increasingly apparent that we *become the way we are perceived* (as perceived by ourselves, and as perceived by others). Feedback within the social system is an important shaper of behavior. Having been given constructive feedback, individuals may see themselves as having inner strengths for handling difficulties and will not be overwhelmed by the intrusion of problems. They may wish that the problems had not arisen, but they will move on through the responsibilities of life in the context of the belief that they have the wherewithal to solve these problems. This attitude toward life's challenges is a fundamental key to the increased independence of older individuals. Medical research states that many physical ailments, aches and pains, have their roots in mental attitudes (Fine, 1973; Goldstein, 1971; Mosak & Dreikurs, 1973).

Those who work with older persons have significant influence in the development of this attitude. If we believe that basically individuals are capable of handling their own lives, this attitude will be picked up in a thousand verbal and nonverbal cues by the elderly. Of course the opposite is true as well. If we secretly believe that individuals need us to take care of them, the cues of belief in their inadequacy will be communicated to the elderly.

We argue that it is the *present* goals within the social system that are significant for interpreting behavior. The present goals are not basically different from those goals that have operated in the past. The behavioral direction of elderly individuals was influenced and shaped at very early periods in the life cycle. However, even at this early period, the behavior is best explained in terms of the child's "purpose" or "goal." This behavioral direction shaped in the early years remains consistent over the life span and may be fairly consistent from one social system to another. Every individual has a basic "behavioral direction," due to his or her patterned choices in response to feedback received. Particular characteristics will vary from individual to individual. The "behavioral direction" represents each individual's learned ways to cope with his or her early environment. These learned ways continue with us into old age, regardless of their present effectiveness or accuracy at interpreting the way our world is constructed. Earlier in this chapter the case study of "Martha" showed her current attention-getting patterns. Martha may well have had parents who were so busy that they did not take time to listen to her in the normal conversational exchanges as a young child. Martha, like other children, learned that parents pay more attention to misbehavior than acceptable behavior. Out of her own early needs to feel secure, to develop a sense of "place" in the world, Martha developed goals of control as her way of trying to establish a sense of "belonging" in the social system. Parental feedback confirmed the pattern.

BELONGING IN THE LATER YEARS

It is unfortunate that most individuals have trained themselves in negative ways to try to guarantee a feeling that they do "belong." The evidence is clear and substantial: We all need to feel we are cared about, that we matter, that we share this earth and therefore are a fundamental part of humanity.

Each of us, young and old alike, must develop a sense of belonging, of place, under the restrictions of the possibilities of our life situation. All human beings throughout the life span sense, to varying degrees, a need to feel that they are cared for, that they matter to *someone*. It is unfortunate that most individuals have trained themselves in negative ways to guarantee a feeling that they do belong. Children learn quickly that people who matter are more likely to pay attention if they misbehave. As adults this same pattern is carried in our heads, except it is more sophisticated now. By the later years individuals have learned to be quite clever in manipulating others to secure some sense of "belonging." Manipulative processes will be especially operative in the later years if they have been the mode of operation in earlier years. Negative manipulation strategies aimed at garnering some feeling of belonging seem better than nothing at all. Unfortunately these negative techniques take their toll by decreasing self-value and confidence. The feedback from others is usually veiled or open rejection. This reaction only escalates the need for stronger control and manipulation in the system.

To intervene in this system is our task. We must not, however, be drawn into a frantic search for an ultimate feeling of "belonging" under the illusion that only this can constructively meet the needs of older persons. This search can be one of the biggest stumbling blocks—one that gets in the way of discovering the survival benefit of those experiences that offer *some degree* of belonging. It is from the day-to-day experiences in which some measure of belonging is present that individuals will find enough support and sense of place to help them perform the constructive behaviors of which they are capable. Once older individuals begin to see themselves as still having something to offer (a feeling that they have a *place*) and to perceive themselves more realistically in relation to others, they will most likely begin to act with more self-confidence and with increased independence.

There are two major sources of belonging: external feedback, in messages of respect we receive from others; internal feedback, from feelings of contribution to various degrees of individual and common needs. When older persons do not receive belonging feedback, not only are their growth and development as individuals arrested, but their relationships with others are crippled. Elderly who experience constructive healthy messages of belonging (with some regularity) will not have to resort to unproductive behavior in their relationships with others. They will be able to contribute positive support to their peers. They will feel better about themselves. Those who work with elderly through various agencies and institutions will find constructive cooperative responses from those older individuals who have a sense of *place.* Therefore, it is to the advantage of elderly persons and professionals who work with them to pay serious attention to the development of a constructive sense of *belonging* in the later years.

ATTITUDES OF THE PROFESSIONAL

That we all need to be a part of a caring relationship, both to give and to receive care, is obvious. What is not so clear is *how* helpful caring is expressed or how to convey healthy feedback that encourages a feeling of belonging and responsible social behavior. A crucial link in the development of a sense of *place* is the development of a healthy attitude of the professional who works with older persons. From the many attitudinal stances of the professional, the one that offers considerable constructive feedback is an attitude that results in *acting in behalf of another person's growth.* This means, essentially, to respond in a healthy way to individuals so as to increase a feeling of belonging is to do those things for them that they cannot do for themselves. Doing things for people that they can do for themselves usually is not acting in a way that will encourage their growth.

When the professional adopts an attitude of doing things for individuals that they could do for themselves, a double message is communicated. It may convey a feeling of caring, but it is the type of caring that does not allow growth. At a deeper level this protective caring communicates mixed messages: Does this mean he thinks I cannot do it as rapidly, as thoroughly, as perfectly as he can do it? Does it establish something about the roles each of us are to assume—that he is the capable one and I am the dependent one? Does it mean he does not trust me? Does it mean he expects me to goof and therefore avoids the mistake by doing it for me? Regardless of which is most pertinent at the time, any of them can recall hosts of gnawing inadequacy feelings in the older person. If this is the predominant pattern of relating, it will lead to the prevalence of inadequate feelings that decrease a sense of belonging. When we lower belonging the stage is set for unproductive behavior patterns to emerge to compensate for feelings of not belonging.

Nash Love, Jr. (1976) calls attention to what he describes as the *love-mistake*, which is made by many professionals. Individuals make the *love-mistake* when they interpret love primarily as continued unconditional acceptance of the individual *and* his or her behavior no matter what the behavior happens to be. Even if the behavior is persistent, unproductive attention getting, if we follow the *love-mistake*, the individual is to be loved (accepted) into changing this behavior. Unfortunately, the acceptance of such behavior reinforces that behavior; that is, it increases the likelihood of its continuing! To avoid the *love-mistake*, it is important to distinguish between acceptance of the individual and acceptance of his or her behavior.

Many individuals have difficulty with the distinction between accepting the individual and accepting the behavior. How, many ask, can you refuse to accept the behavior without communicating rejection of the person? If the definition of caring previously described in this chapter—*acting in behalf of another person's growth*—is accepted, this concern can be handled with more confidence. By *not* accepting, for example, unproductive attention getting, the behavior is not reinforced, and with continued lack of reinforcement the behavior should gradually disappear (Blackman & Silberman, 1975). By helping to extinguish unproductive behavior, the counselor has acted toward the individual with genuine caring, the type that acts to enhance his or her increased sense of belonging.

To care genuinely means to grant endurance assistance to the individual—something he cannot do for himself. Jim, 68, is learning to walk with crutches following the surgical removal of his left leg. If Jim is to continue to grow and develop, he will need to learn to walk with crutches. Even though it has been many months since the recovery from surgery, Jim complains and resists the process of walking with the crutches. How can Jim be genuinely cared for? How can endurance assistance be bestowed? One approach would be to work with Jim on techniques for walking with crutches and as soon as he has demonstrated a capacity to handle the crutches, refuse to carry him or feel sorry for him (i.e., refuse to make *love-mistake*). The genuine care Jim needs is for someone to encourage him by words and, more important, by actions.

There are at least two typical responses to Jim that create discouragement. One of these is to feel sorry for him and do his walking for him, either by carrying him or going to great lengths to minimize the need for walking. This is immediately appealing because it seems the easiest way out, but it is feedback that reinforces dependence. Jim would probably do a lot to encourage this himself especially if he receives "payoff" for not coming to grips with the crutches. The price Jim would pay in loss of courage and feelings of belonging would begin to emerge in other areas of his life. Feeling sorry for others and the attendant rescue of them from assuming responsibility for much of their own life foster dependence and a low sense of belonging. Continually rescued individuals have little chance to develop their potential or feel they are sharing this crust of the earth, pulling their part of the load. Consequently they are less likely to feel that they belong.

Another approach that helps to reinforce discouragement in Jim is to neglect or ignore him. It would be easy to give up on him, to let him stew in his own complaining. His resistance is not yet attractive and might be seen by some as only the tip of the iceberg, a problem so enormous that they do not want to get involved. If one is operating from a "cause" orientation to behavior, then this case might well appear to be too tough to handle. Further, if one understands caring from the point of view of doing things *for* people, then getting involved may very well signal demands of such magnitude that Jim himself may end up being ignored. Whatever the reason for neglect, it has a most unsettling effect on an individual's sense of belonging.

Most individuals are not aware of the *love-mistake*. They are not used to thinking how unhealthy it is to relate consistently toward older persons by doing things for them that they can do for themselves. If Jim is to be moved toward more responsibility for his own walking, it will be necessary to intervene in the system. The feedback will have to be changed, which will in turn affect Jim's interaction. His wife, children, friends, and part-time nurse were instructed to say to him about the crutches, "I think you can handle them, Jim," and do just that. No one was to say anything resembling "isn't it awful that you are in such a condition," or "isn't it terrible that this has happened to you and it is so tough for you to get around." After Jim had demonstrated his ability to get around on the crutches, he still complained some. The goal of his behavior was, no doubt, to finally manipulate some "soft heart" into rescuing him. Strict instructions were given to avoid doing the walking for him, and *expect* him to do his own walking. In two months Jim was walking up stairs and taking walks outside —something he never expected to accomplish. He had recovered, at age 68, a significant amount of lost courage. He became much more cheerful, cooperative, and seemed to demonstrate increased feelings of belonging. Without this approach Jim could easily have backed into a life-style of disengagement. Instead he was enabled to develop his potential, and his response to a realistic experience of aging became one of continued activity. Important to Jim's fulfillment of his potential were some important background factors. He was fortunate enough to have had the barriers in his home corrected so that his walking aids would not encounter problems. He had good medical care. His diet was more than adequate, and guided exercise was available. Counseling was effective because the intervention took into account the stress-filled social situation, Jim's interaction and feedback.

RESPONSIBILITY THROUGHOUT THE LIFE SPAN

As the attitude of the professional turned from doing *for* Jim to one of encouraging him to develop his own potential, a dormant sense of responsibility began to emerge. We cannot economically afford to allow the potential of older persons to lie fallow and gradually atrophy. One assumption underlying intervention into the social system is that independence for elders does not mean freedom *from* responsibility but freedom *to* healthy responsibility. It is in this freedom throughout the life span to assume responsibility for oneself and for others that healthy personalities develop.

One significant result of Jim's experience, which resulted in a willingness to help himself and others, appeared to verify the interrelatedness of freedom and responsibility. Prior to his accomplishment with the crutches Jim was continually concerned with and absorbed in his own problems. His life was increasingly turned in on himself. This is primarily the reflection of extreme discouragement fostered by being felt sorry for by well-intentioned persons. They thought they were helping by adopting a basic attitude of doing things *for* older persons.

Jim's awakening concern for others represents additional growth benefits from an increased feeling of belonging: a willingness to care for others and contribute positively toward their achieving a feeling of belonging. In spite of this positive movement, there is one danger here to which we should be alerted. Jim needs to be gently guided toward doing for others those things that they cannot do for themselves. The temptation during this flowering period is for Jim to be so proud of himself that he will try to do too much for others. He will be drawn into making the same *love-mistake* with his peers. We would not want to discourage Jim's newly emerging concern, but neither would we want him to discourage others' potential growth in responsibility by taking away opporunities for them to grow. He must be taught the skill of constructive feedback, that is, not doing for others what they can do for themselves.

Family members unwittingly tend to expect older persons to be inadequate in assuming responsibility for their own affairs of life. One of the authors happened to be talking with a 92-year-old lady and suddenly realized how loud he was talking. Just to check for volume needed, the voice was gradually lowered to a soft conversational tone. The 92-year-old was picking up every word (no hearing aid)! We communicate so many messages that we *expect* inferior functioning. One of the central themes that we need to start communicating to older persons is that we expect them to assume more responsibility for themselves and others. For most of us this will require reprogramming *our* brain so that it is more natural for us to assume that the elderly too are capable of using a greater proportion of their potential.

Older persons obviously have a lot to give in the growth of others. Unfortunately, when they show evidences of giving or helping others we tend to suggest that they may be overexerting or that they may need someday the gift they are about to bestow on another.

> Dee, 76 years of age and in good health, offered to babysit for the weekend while her daughter and her husband attended an out-of-town class reunion. "I just don't want you to be worn down by the children, Mother. They are such a drain. It would be better if you had the weekend to catch up on your rest."
>
> "But I feel fine, and the children are not that much of a problem," Mother insisted.
>
> "I am sure you feel OK now, but you forget how easily you tire out, Mother," her daughter insisted.

The message coming through to Dee from her daughter are these: Your helping days are virtually over; you have very little to give to others; get used to the position of dependence. Dee's daughter would be horrified to think she would ever directly communicate anything like this. Most of us would feel the same, and yet our feedback betrays our best intentions.

In a few of the world's societies where there are exceptionally high proportions of older persons living to be more than 100 years of age, we find that responsibility expectations of the elderly remain high throughout the life span. In the Georgian province in southern Russia, a 98-year-old man not only gathers tea leaves during the annual harvest, it is *expected* of him. In another part of this province, in the high Caucasus Mountains section the elderly scramble down a steep, half-mile-long trail to swim and bathe in a chilly stream. For most of one man's 104 years he has taken a daily swim, winter and summer, in this stream. Alexander Leaf, who reported on the long-livers in *National Geographic* (January 1973), admitted that he was amazed at the exertion by a man over 100, but found the level of physical activity among all the old people to be high. The Hunzas of Kashmir and the villagers of Vilcambamba in Ecuador also had an unusual number of very rigorous old folk climbing over the steep slopes of the mountainous country that is home to them. No one felt sorry for these old people. There was no trying to talk them out of physical activity. The long life of these individuals is a kind of marvel. But Alexander Leaf was more impressed with the physical fitness of the older individuals than with their age.

It is not just prolonging life that is the important issue. Improving the quality of life and enhancing independence and the potential for contributions are primary. There are numerous examples of individuals who defy the traditions of society. Leopold Stokowski, one of the great musical conductors, signed a six-year recording contract with a London studio at age 95. Dickenson (1973) catalogs numerous such feats. Picasso seemed to approach his full powers in his 90s. Pablo Casals was still performing at 95. Titian was killed by a plague at 99 while still actively painting. Grandma Moses painted her last picture at 101. Eden Philpott published a novel at 96. Bertrand Russell published his last novel at 91, Santayana at 87, John Dewey at 87. Thomas Hobbes translated *The Iliad* and *The Odyssey* at 88.

In the political world Ho Chi Minh died while head of state at 79. Mao Tse-Tung was in his 80s when death took him from his position of leadership. De Gaulle quit at 78, Churchill at 80, Lord Addison (House of Lords) at 82. Lord Chancellor Halsburgy served as a judge in the House of Lords until age 93. Theodore Francis Green left the United States Senate at 93. El Mokji, Grand Vizier of Morocco at age 104, had a long career in which he dealt with both Napoleon III and representatives from President Eisenhower. The description of Justice Holmes in his ninetieth year is most inspiring. He had been a judge for 50 years, 30 years a member of the Supreme Court, widowed, no children, but remaining involved with his work. He quoted these lines on his ninetieth birthday, "Death tugs at my ear and says, 'Live: I am coming,'" (Dickenson, p. 4).

It will not be the advancements of medical science and technology, as important as they are, that will make the significant contributions toward increased independence of older persons in our culture. When we change our basic assumptions about aging, we will begin to see significant strides toward independence. It is an exciting potential.

SUMMARY

There is increasing evidence that most older individuals have the ability to develop their potential in many physical, mental, and emotional areas. However, many older individuals seem to display more unproductive than healthy behavior. To understand the meaning of the older individual's behavior, it is important to look for the purpose or goal of the behavior within the social system. A guide for interpreting the specific goals of unproductive behavior involves four levels: Attention-gaining, Bossy, Counter-hurt, and Disablement. Knowing the goals of unproductive behavior and even how to change that behavior is only half the task. Continued growth is dependent on a growing sense of belonging and self-respect. Constructive feedback from the professional involves doing things for the elderly that they cannot do for themselves and refusing to do for them what they can manage. This attitude represents a crucial link in the process of developing a sense of belonging, and, ultimately, of prolonged independence.

Chapter 4
Procedures for Intervention in the Social System of the Elderly

In the preceding chapter a social systems model was developed that offers alternative directions for understanding aging in our culture. This framework offers a counseling approach with a goal toward adaptation to the elderly process, the prevention of debilitating maladaptive behaviors, and the fortifying of aging individuals with the capacity to enjoy life right up to the end.

The intention of the preceding chapter was to describe the dynamics of a social systems approach that interprets the individual's behavior within a social situation. In this chapter the focus is on strategies for intervening in the social system to increase the adaptation to aging, to circumvent feedback that reinforces unproductive maladaptive behavior, and to support positive responsible behavior.

The intervention strategies will apply to older persons in noninstitutional and institutional settings. Their application may vary slightly between individuals who live alone and those who live with a partner (Chapter 7) and also between those who require greater levels of care. Processes for intervention may not differ for elderly who live in institutional settings who are relatively independent and those who live in their own homes with family members or a spouse. Case studies (Chapter 6) will also reflect individuals who reside in independent residences as well as in institutional settings.

THE EFFECTS OF INDIVIDUAL ATTITUDES AND BELIEFS ON INTERACTION

Particular personality integration will affect the way an elderly individual responds in a social system. Whether an individual sees problems as unfair impositions that make life unbearable or as unfortunate but manageable will affect his or her interaction and subsequent feedback. If the beliefs in injustice predominate, we can predict that the individual will probably interact in ways that avoid responsible behavior on his or her part. If the feedback he gets reinforces his avoidance, the system can be said to become functionally unbalanced. On the other hand, if his beliefs are that problems can be managed, chances are that responsible behavior will be displayed and thus the system remains functionally balanced. There will more than likely be varying degrees of responsibility and avoidance at different times and depending on the nature of the problems faced. The degree of imbalance will vary as well.

Our attitudes and beliefs about ourselves will affect our response in the social system. Intervention with an individual can be seen as a systems intervention since change in the individual's behavior will affect the feedback he receives from others in his social system.

For most individuals there is a continuing inclination to run themselves down, to belittle their abilities, and to deny publicly any ownership of competency. This is internal feedback that can be used for avoidance. The first task of the older person who wishes to develop as a more independent person is self-intervention in his own personal system, that is, overcoming these negative attitudes. Every time we have a negative, pessimistic thought about ourselves we need to imagine a huge STOP sign in our heads and ask ourselves, "Is this trip necessary?" If an individual finds it difficult to give up the negative self-talk, then he or she must be getting reinforcing feedback for it. Is there a desire to get out of a task or responsibility related to the negative self-talk? Does the individual need to feel self-pity to avoid social responsibility? There are other more constructive ways to cope with life.

This negative self-talk has its origin largely in misunderstood religious teachings that exhort individuals to "deny themselves." This has been interpreted, too often, to mean the individual's religious duty is not only to deny himself but to hate himself. This has spawned a mistaken notion that to be humble the person must never admit to himself, and above all, never to others, that he possesses strengths, or the extent to which successes were due to his skills. This popular notion serves to undermine self-confidence. It emphasizes inadequacy and hinders growth as an independent person. In contrast to this, an often overlooked teaching in Christianity emphasizes valuing oneself. The early writers of the Bible put it like this, "The whole law summed up in one phrase is this: 'Love your neighbor *like you love yourself.*'" The message is clear. Two thousand years ago, insight about the development of independent persons existed. The process for fulfilling the basic commandment of caring for the neighbor is understood to pivot on whether you are skilled in loving and valuing yourself. Development as a responsible social participant rides on willingness to change the negative self-talk. The older person who escapes from the slavery of his or her own negative self-talk is an individual with a free mind, on the road to increased independence. Often others see this individual as a genius! But that rarity need not be the case. There is within each one of us this same potential waiting for its release. Walt Whitman, in *Leaves of Grass*, describes this potential that even the animal kingdom shares:

> I think I could turn and live with animals, they
> are so placid and self-contained;
> I stand and look at them long and long.
> They do not sweat and whine about their condition.
> They do not lie awake in the dark and weep for
> their sins;
> They do not make me sick discussing their duty to God.
> Not one is dissatisfied, not one is demented with the
> mania of owning things.
> Not one kneels to another, nor to his kind that lived
> thousands of years ago.
> Not one is respectable or industrious over the
> whole earth.

A second step, of great importance for becoming a more self-confident independent older person, involves what Rudolph Dreikurs (1964) calls declaring an immediate "cease-fire" with ourselves! Most individuals, especially during the latter part of the life span, fight with themselves about habits they want to break or about motivation for doing daily tasks or maintaining social contacts. It is assumed that the only way to control ourselves is to fight ourselves. Older people know they should do something, but how can they motivate themselves to begin? That is the reason for the continuous fighting. It is seen as a motivator to make older persons do what they do not want to do. In other words, we arbitrarily split ourselves into two persons: one that wants to do the good thing and the second that wants to do the bad. The elderly engage in a practice of endlessly watching over themselves to see if they will do the right thing or the wrong thing. They will feel proud if they have done the right thing and will blame themselves for doing the wrong thing. They can always use the internal dilemma to push them toward inaction. This pattern is based on the assumption, according to Dreikurs, that every person consists of two distinct parts: good and bad, rational and irrational, emotion and reason.

We threaten and punish ourselves just like teachers threaten and punish students who will not study or behave. This approach rarely works on either the elderly or on children. Intimidation to coax ourselves into behaving does not show much faith in ourselves. Independence will not be very compatible with this view of ourselves. Independence would always hinge on whether or not the individual succeeded or failed. Whether he or she was up or down, good or bad.

Independence as a person requires another perspective, a view of ourselves as a whole person. This one (not two) person has the ability to do anything, good or bad, rational or irrational. Dreikurs argues that these seeming paradoxical behaviors are only different aspects of one and the same being. The ambivalent internal feedback created from the struggle, should I do this or should I do that, is seen as an arrangement with a *purpose*. It may be used to avoid responsibility, to demand that others take care of the individual, or to pretend forward responsible movement while actually preventing such movement. There may be many reasons why the individual prefers not to decide, but the result is always the same. This is a little like the individual who frequently invites others to come visit, but he never actually sets a time. Others, not aware they have been taken in, often remark that he or she is *so* friendly.

Guilt operates much in the same vein. Suppose the older person feels guilty about something he has done. What he does not realize is that while he is concerned with remorse over what he has done in the past, he cannot address himself to present responsibilities. Guilt feelings are often the expression of good intentions which individuals really do not have. They are pretenses. An anonymous twelfth-century theologian suggested that if an individual has done something for which he is sorry, feeling guilty is not appropriate. Getting on with one's responsibilities and resolving to try to avoid the behavior next time is the called-for behavior. Consumed by guilt, the individual is hindered from considering what needs to be done *now*. The older person suffering from guilt is very likely avoiding some present task. By feeling guilty, persons try to impress others and themselves with high moral standards without any need to *do anything*.

If Dreikurs' assumption is true, then it logically follows that the elderly are not the victims of their emotions but may have helped to create them. Individuals decide what pattern of behavior they want to follow and work up emotions to justify those intentions. This is not a concept readily embraced by individuals of any age. There is good reason. We do not like to admit that we are the master of our own emotions. It is easier to accept an idea that suggests persons are driven by their emotions. Then the individual is not responsible for his own behavior. Emotions can then make his decisions for him.

It is not easy to declare a cease-fire within ourselves and begin to assume responsibility for our own behavior. Most individuals have been trained to look at themselves as victims of circumstances, such as genetic destiny, irrational forces within and without, family and social background, and so on. The elderly are easily seen as victims of society. This approach in no way is intended to urge acceptance of society's second-rate treatment of old people. Each older person can decide how he or she will respond to a world that offers much second-rate treatment.

Victor Frankl (1963), a Jewish psychiatrist, argued that individuals have more control over their responses to circumstances than they realize. He wrote about the issue of meaning to life in the midst of a German concentration camp during World War II. During this experience, individuals were stripped of any external support from previous status, possessions, background, or experience. Each day brought continual humiliation. Every hour was lived out under the threat of death. Under these circumstances it might be more difficult to deny that individuals are victims of society. It was precisely here, however, in the midst of such inhuman conditions, that Frankl concluded that no matter what the circumstances, there is one last freedom that cannot be taken from the individual, the *freedom to decide how he will respond to his circumstances.* We can respond as victims or as creators of our own actions, but in either case, we have decided.

When the individual is understood in terms of interacting in a social system, it becomes more apparent that he is a decision-making organism. The elderly decide every step they take, although not always on a conscious level: what emotions are useful, what demands to deny, what responsibility to undermine. These are all decided by individuals. But they can also decide that they have a profound sense of place, of belonging, when they do what has to be done, cooperate with others, contribute, and participate.

This is a revolutionary idea. It means individuals are deciding persons, active in choices that have bearing on their own lives. This is the stuff of which confidence and independence is made: *to never quit. Never!*

Support for this determination of older persons to assume more responsibility in their own lives comes from the important concept of acceptance of themselves as they are. Many elderly harbor unrealistic views of themselves, and very few would be willing to agree that they are good enough as they are. The fact is, however, that individuals have good reason to be satisfied with themselves. This means that although, of course, humans make mistakes, this does not justify dissatisfaction. To make mistakes is part of our heritage as humans. It is impossible to be perfect, and even striving toward perfection makes no sense because it is an unattainable goal. No matter what we do, there will always be a feeling that we could have done better. So why not accept ourselves as we are and give others the same acceptance? Many feel to accept themselves as they are would mean stagnation and cessation of growth. Striving for perfection, even though it is patently unattainable, becomes a kind of carrot on a stick dangling in front of us but always just beyond our grasp. This refusal to give up perfection manifests a disturbing view of human nature: The human organism basically, if not continually motivated externally, moves toward stagnation, atrophy, and ultimately death. Any innate growth stimulus is thus denied. One need look no further than the developing infant for counterevidence. The young child's insatiable curiosity and unquenchable desire to explore, without carrots dangling before him, tell us that humans have a natural motivation to grow, to learn, to explore. There is considerable evidence that shows older persons can grow, can learn for the enjoyment of learning.

To accept oneself as one is requires a profound self-respect. This acceptance is not to be confused with boastful pride. Arrogant pride represents the attempt to be "more than one in fact is," just as uninformed humility is the attempt to achieve status by appearing to be "less than one in fact is." To accept oneself as one is only means we are what we are and we can like ourselves as we are. We are not superhumans; we make mistakes and have faults. We have strengths and weaknesses that qualify us for citizenship in the human race. We can choose to accept ourselves as we are in the confidence of our natural drives toward growth. To older individuals who may feel much pressure to prove their worth because of age, this different way of thinking about themselves can bring significant relief. This pressure can be like a heavy burden toward which older persons must direct much of their energy that could have been used for more independent living.

For some, life seems always to be characterized by trying to *push back the tide.* For this person, "never giving up" brings unfortunate results. It is like the swimmer caught in a riptide. The tendency is to frantically try to swim against the current. This can easily result in drowning. If instead the swimmer goes with the riptide current, it will usually push him on down the beach and out of the narrow confines of the current so that he can swim to shore. The secret is to know when to keep trying and when to ride out the riptide.

If older persons are to make significant progress toward intervening in their own internal feedback they must cease putting themselves down and begin reinforcing their potential through a genuine caring for themselves. They must stop fighting with themselves, give up the perfection seeking, and start accepting themselves as they are. Older persons have tremendous potential. They have to discover this strength in themselves by letting it come from within. It is there. With their years of experience and wisdom, they have the potential for knowing better than most when to stick it out and when to go with the current. These intervention strategies allow the individual to operate with greater freedom and independence within the normal life context over longer time spans.

THE COMING OF DEMOCRACY

The growth in independence and freedom of older Americans must of necessity take place within the larger societal system with all the restraints and possibilities of that society. Society is usually thought of as contributing negative pressures on older people. However, there is let loose in our culture a force rapidly gaining momentum that offers a supportive context for increased freedom and independence for the elderly. This development is the increasing democratization of society.

For centuries the unwritten structure of many parts of society had determined that "parents are superior to children," "men are superior to women," "the rich are superior to the poor," and "whites are superior to blacks," and in recent decades, the "young are superior to the old." However, the growing perception of the meaning of democracy and its effects upon interpersonal relationships has profoundly changed many aspects of these relationships. The evolutionary movement for children's rights has culminated in society's increased awareness, if not acceptance, of the rights of children (e.g., the United Nations' declaration of 1979 as the "Year of the Child"). The "civil rights" movement of the 1960s has done much toward breaking down the myth of white supremacy. The "women's rights" movement, gaining further momentum in the 1980s, will establish that women have as equal claims as men to dignity, respect, and access to opportunities. In the wings, the next crusade may well be the awakening of the elderly to claims of equality. The elderly have been most timid in past decades. This new context will offer encouragement in the struggle for greater independence.

The evolution of democracy has encompassed a long history of movement away from rule over others by kings to the signing of the

Magna Carta, which placed kings under the law. Seeds of social equality were sown during the French and American Revolutions and the Civil War to the present time. The harvest that is now being gleaned by numbers of individuals in this society involves the coming of age of individuals: laying equal claim to respect, justice, and access to opportunity. The implication of this growth is that democracy is not just a political promise but a *way of life*. It is largely the impact of democracy that is transforming our social institutions and is raising some questions about the traditional approaches to dealing with the elderly.

Many people today, especially those who have to work directly with the elderly, tend to upset themselves about the notion that the old are their social equals. They say to themselves: They cannot be my social equal; chaos would result if we did not act for them, make decisions for them; besides, how can they know what is best for them; we, obviously, know more than they about what is best for them. This is the crux of a common mistake made about equality. In reality, equality in knowledge, experience, or skill is not the issue. These have never indicated equality. Is an individual with a bachelor's degree "more equal" than a high school graduate? Does a master's degree make an individual "more equal" than a person with a bachelor's degree? Or is the possession of a doctorate "more equal" than all? Obviously not; more enviable perhaps, but not "more equal."

Equality here means that people, regardless of their individual distinctions, share equal claims to dignity and respect. The belief that the young are superior to the old comes from our cultural heritage: that individuals are inferior or superior according to their birth, money, sex, color, and age.

The "Gray Panther" organization reflects one focus of national concern for equal claims of respect, dignity and access to opportunity for older individuals. Many older persons who have remained silent are beginning to realize that theirs is a cause whose time has arrived. They see their unequal treatment as intolerable and are increasingly unwilling to submit to autocratic, dominant-submissive relationships. Those who work with older persons are vaguely sensing that some older persons are beginning to demand equal respect and dignity and, consequently these workers feel they must begin lowering the autocratic profile. At the same time those who are comfortable only with an autocratic approach to the elderly may not be familiar with current methods based on more democratic principles. Consequently these professionals who work with older persons are in a dilemma. Simple solutions and shortcuts just do not exist. If we are to function as motivators for the elderly in a democratic context, *our attitudes* must change.

Attempts at democratic techniques while still holding onto autocratic attitudes will be interpreted by older individuals as an unwillingness to grant older persons the full claim to equal dignity and respect. Older people are very perceptive. They can pick up on nondemocratic cues, however well meaning our intentions. Increasingly, we will find older people rebelling more openly at our patronizing methods. Those professionals who are successful with older persons will be those who act out democratic attitudes.

Older people are watching our "feet" more and our words less. We must stop relying on talking a good line and get with the changing social context if we are to be helpful as counselors to the old. The democratic realities are the wave of the only future we can see. To be respected and treated with dignity have always been the substructure of healthy individuals. We ignore this context today at our peril.

THE CARE-GIVER ROLE

The task of encouragement with older persons will involve individuals at different levels of professional development. Individuals of various ages will be able to make useful contributions toward this goal. The usual categories of distinctions (professionals, nonprofessionals, or paraprofessionals) do not seem particularly useful in describing those who are capable of communicating encouragement. In many respects the elderly themselves have significant potential for transmitting encouragement to their peers. Certainly, one does not have to be a professional to be capable of contributing to the growing freedom of older persons. The most appropriate criterion seems to be the ability of individuals to care about the growth and development of old people. Therefore, when describing those who are potentially capable of counseling older persons, we will assume the role of "care-giver" to include a spouse, relative, friend, or professional.

Before the care-giver begins solo therapy with the elderly, appropriate course work and practicum field work is a necessity.

For any care-giver in practicum who has a client pool of elderly persons, it is important to get qualified supervision. If a qualified supervisor who works with the elderly is not available, the most closely allied source is a marriage and/or family therapist. Often clinical psychologists, clinical social workers, and psychiatric nurses who are active in counseling older persons could serve well as supervisors.

Taping counseling sessions, preferably video, but certainly audio, are very important for supervision. Obtaining the client's permission to tape is essential. Usually this presents no difficulty. The ideal is to have supervision from behind a one-way mirror, but this is often difficult to work out.

A NEW CONCEPT OF CARING

A strategy of caring that is appropriate today must rid itself of paternalistic characteristics. Caring that draws attention to the care-giver's superior position or ability to care, that does those things for people that they can do for themselves, that fosters dependency upon the care-giver, and that encourages a feeling of indebtedness to the care-giver is paternalistic in nature. This kind of caring will not be helpful for individuals who are surrounded by a society increasingly structured for protecting the individual rights of all its citizens.

Even the concept of caring must be redefined in ways that bring it into the mainstream of an evolving democratic society. The care-giver's concern under this approach then is to encourage the growth and expression of the older individual's capacities and to avoid feedback that reinforces dependency and avoidance.

One basic prerequisite to intervention in the social system of the elderly individual is to make sure the older person can perform the activity or task in question. One way to determine this is to role-play the task at a time other than when the responsibility is expected. (The reason for this is to avoid reinforcing one of the levels of unproductive behavior that may be operating.) Through observations of the older persons their baseline activity can be decribed. One elderly woman insisted that she no longer had the strength in her hands to lift her plate of food over to her table. The older woman was unaware that she had been observed moving a portable TV set from the floor, where it was inconvenient for her to watch, up to a small table for better viewing. Thus she obviously could lift her plate, but evidently she had not been getting positive reinforcement for this behavior. More reinforcement had been received for her unproductive behavior. There will be times when care-givers will have to "sit on their hands" to avoid intervening in areas where the older person is capable but may be slower or less efficient. And, on the other side of this issue, the care-giver (spouse, relative, friend, or professional) must be prepared to receive a lot of "flak." The older person did not get to the point overnight of manipulating others to do things for them that they could be doing for themselves. When intervention occurs, things may get "worse" before they get better. They may well pull out all the stops in order to keep the care-giver busy with them: tears, protests, accusations, and so on.

DOES A PROBLEM EXIST?

Before a care-giver makes choices about the kind of technique(s) that might be useful in dealing with problems that thwart movement of the other person toward greater independence, it is necessary to decide whether a problem actually exists. Some simple rules exist for making a determination: (1) What is the frequency of the questionable behavior? (2) Does the behavior hurt the individual or others? (3) Does the behavior hinder a healthy adaptation to life and the individual's immediate social circumstances? It is quite possible that the behavior in question is seen as a problem because of a rigid, uninformed stance of the care-giver. One staff person complained that a nursing home resident was uncooperative. The resident argued that the staff treated residents as children, and she "was not about to participate in the behavior suggested by the staff person—using crayons in coloring books." The need for care facilities and trained staff for the elderly has risen faster than the ability to produce competent care-givers. The attraction of profits in elderly care facilities has also kept nursing home administrators from getting and keeping trained staff.

Many individuals have been attracted into the field because it is new and offers immediate financial opportunities. It will be a while before the necessary criteria are developed and implemented that will assure older persons of good nursing home care. Until that time we will continue to be shocked at what passes for care with respect to older persons. One of the chief problems that recurs in a thousand ways is this: Elderly persons are intuitively seen as "children," treated like children, and then chided for acting like "children" after all this reinforcement. One elderly resident showed an inclination toward dolls, and on occasion after occasion the staff reinforced this behavior, thereby unwittingly training the older person to retreat into childhood. There just may be a time when the older person is right, that the problem may well lie with the individual staff rather than the older individual.

ENCOURAGING WORDS

Some encouraging processes to accompany interventions that are democratic in nature are quite simple and easy to put into practice. These will be encouraging to elderly in and out of institutional settings. They involve a meshing of our words with actions, both of which incite respect and cooperation. Instead of "telling" (autocratic associations) Martha to close her door when she is watching TV, we suggest asking, "Would you be willing (democratic associations) to close your door while you are watching TV?" We are not so naive as to believe that this will guarantee that the door will close. Frequent reinforcing feedback for unproductive behavior will not be overcome by one statement. But, we argue, that the "would you be willing" statements may begin to win cooperative response patterns. This form of motivation does not imply a boss telling an inferior person what to do. It says in effect, I *cannot tell* you what to do. I cannot order you around. I respect your right to make choices and assume that if you are respected, you will be more willing to make choices that guarantee respect for others.

When we *tell* others to do something, we are opening ourselves to subtle and open rebellion. In the future we can count on this increasing. We must open ourselves to motivation processes that respect the dignity and worth of individuals.

We can use this democratic phrase in the routine daily interactions involving communication with older persons. A middle-aged daughter may be tempted to respond to her elderly mother like this, "You always want me to take you grocery shopping when I am swamped with work." This implies criticism which is neither constructive nor respectful of a person's equal claims to dignity. It further implies the person who asked is inferior for not knowing better than to ask at inappropriate times. This is the "stuff" of human relationships that builds resentment and uncooperativeness. It is the kind of reinforcing feedback that maintains maladaptive behavior in family systems. The older person has every right to ask to be taken grocery shopping. Knowing better techniques for asking and responding are ways of intervening in the system. A more appropriate response might go something like, "I am willing to take you grocery shopping when I finish my work, which will be about 5:00 P.M." Or better still, we could be even more responsive to equal claims of respect by working out, *ahead*, times that would be set aside for grocery shopping. This arrangement, making use of the "I am willing" prefix, lifts the older person out of the bind of never being sure whether she can count on being able to go shopping and whether she is valued enough to be taken seriously. Planning ahead of time implies, "I respect you enough to take the time to work out an arrangement that is agreeable with you and acceptable to my schedule." It circumvents reinforcement of unproductive behavior.

Other encouraging words that we could benefit from memorizing are: "How would it be . . . ?" Instead of "Helen, you are always taking over the group. Let some others have a chance," as, "Helen, *how would it be* with you if we rotated leadership responsibilities in the groups?" Or, instead of *telling* another person what time a meeting is going to be held, ask, "When would be a good time for you? I am willing to meet any day except Monday and the weekend between 1:30 P.M. and 4:30 P.M."

Further, we can intervene in the social system and begin to build positive encouragement in older persons by refusing to feel sorry for them when they are given responsibilities. We can discourage them and erode their courage by rescuing them, letting them off the hook because they are old, or because we think the expectation might tire them.

If an older person has been given an opportunity to participate in deciding when a meeting is to be held, for example, and then forgets it, do not communicate that you feel sorry for him or her (this carries a hidden message that implies that you expect elderly people to forget). Rather, let the older person bear the consequences of the missed meeting. Always with the attitude, we will try again. When older persons ask for "feel-sorry-for-me" feedback, we do well to practice saying "I believe you can do it" or "You can handle it." If we repeat either one of these more than once or twice with respect to the particular issue at hand, however, the older person may well pick up an underlying lack of confidence. He will sense it if we "protest too much" that there is doubt that they can handle it! If we need to repeat the encouraging phrase too often at one situation, they will suspect that there must be something involved in the task that is more than can be handled or we would not be having to go to such great lengths to try to be convincing. If you believe the older person can handle the situation say it once and ignore any repeated protests, groans, or other clever attempts to escape responsibility.

INTERVENTION WITH SCHEDULES CAN BE ENCOURAGING

There is a kind of popular notion among many that spontaneity is the most valued of attributes. When schedules are suggested, they often draw a lot of negative responses. Unfortunately, to some people schedules conjure up feelings of impersonalness, lack of warmth, and caring. This may come from our society's "love affair" with the *romantic myth* of spontaneity. Many marriages are needlessly strained by holding to the myth that the highest and best love is always spontaneous, that if a person really loves someone he or she will be able to spontaneously (and magically) *know* the other's needs and meet them. This myth is a cruel hoax. No one can magically read another person's mind or that person's particular immediate configuration of needs. To lay this expectation on other persons is to set them up with odds impossible to meet. Perhaps we cling to the myth because it can be purposive in our social system. If another person cannot meet the impossible expectation, we store this evidence and use it as an excuse for not fulfilling *our* responsibilities. We have an excuse. Spontaneity can be nice, but to insist on it can be a way to avoid responsibility in a relationship. On the other hand, schedules can help build caring relationships. Schedules give individuals confidence because they *know* what to expect and count on. They do not have to guess, wonder, or imagine what might be happening in the relationship. We do not mean to suggest that every caring act be scheduled. Heaven forbid. Let us keep spontaneity. In families where older persons reside, however, let us be sure to schedule enough opportunities for communicating and sharing that the older individual can feel he or she can count on these relation-building experiences. They will lower the need for adopting manipulative controlling methods in order to gain attention. Regular times for sharing, for doing something together (read, take a walk, go to a movie, etc.) should be worked out democratically. One sequence might go like this:

> Would you be interested in having a special outing once a week?
> How much time would you think we would need? I would be interested and would be willing to spend up to two hours on the afternoon or evening we decide.
> How would you feel about two hours? Does that seem adequate?
> Which afternoon/evening would be best for you? Friday or Wednesday would be OK for me.
> Which would be your choice?

This same procedure can be used for relieving uncertainty about other needs older people have. It is a good procedure that older married couples should follow with each other. Grocery shopping, going to the beauty parlor, visiting friends, shopping for clothes, and so on, can be scheduled; and care should be taken, once the schedule is set up, to allow only an emergency to interrupt. This does not mean spontaneous experiences may never ever occur now that schedules are put in practice. Whatever both feel like doing outside the schedule is fine. The crucial point is that certain things are scheduled and therefore can be counted on.

INTERVENTION THROUGH ENCOURAGEMENT PROCESSES

One of the most significant techniques for communicating encouragement and good feelings about an individual is through "touching." Touching is "making contact," which has high potential for breaking through interpersonal barriers in many people. To touch another person communicates warmth, caring, and a good feeling about the other person's body. This is especially significant for older individuals.

From our youth culture we hear in a thousand ways that when the skin is wrinkled and dry it is unattractive and even repulsive. The tendency then is to avoid usual touching with older individuals, and this communicates heavy messages to the aging person: If the outer self is a "turn-off," the whole self is at best, questionable. Touching the hands, stroking the arms, hugging the older individual can break through many withdrawn individuals who have concluded they no longer are attractive enough to be worth receiving care.

A second encouragement process involves learning how to listen.

Being "listened to" has a way of restoring an older person's sense of worth. This probably works because to be listened to implies that what the person is saying is important enough to be listened to and the connection is made, "I, therefore, am worth something to someone." However, most of us have had little training in how to listen. Most educational programs have courses for developing skills in speaking. Few courses are available for listening. Because of the scarcity of "listeners" our culture pays the professional listener (therapist) for these services. No matter what our professional training or our age may be, most individuals can learn how to listen. This involves paying attention to what older people are saying through their words, voice tone, gestures, and body posture. Even without direct counseling training, much encouragement can be contributed by listening. Some insist that they do not know what to *say* or what to *tell* a person. Unfortunately, we commonly associate counseling with "telling." We need to see counseling more in terms of skillful listening. Many older people need only to have someone listen to them. Only they can solve their own problems, make their own decisions. Listening helps persons to be able to solve their problems. The dynamics go something like this: If the older person has to make the problem clear enough to be comprehended by the "listener," it will have also become more clear and organized in the older person's head. This clarity helps in problem solving.

It must be said that there are times when listening might not be appropriate. If an older person is engaging in a manipulative quest for feedback that reinforces unproductive behavior, it is better, "out of respect for oneself," to not reinforce this behavior by staying and listening. Perhaps it is better to leave the situation and be ready to listen at a time when the individual is willing to be more rational.

An attitude that intuitively "believes" in the older person is most helpful for preserving independence. Our habits, which involve thinking about aging as a dependency period, can be changed. We have *learned* these responses. We can *learn* new responses to take their place. One specific practice we can begin immediately is to avoid the continual "reminders" we give to older persons. How does reminding affect the individual? Usually the immediate reaction is that most tend to like it. The reason they like it is the problem. They can avoid the responsibility of thinking for themselves. They now have a "servant" who will assume responsibility for them. Well, so what? What is wrong with having a "servant"?

It is not so much a question of anything being wrong as it is an issue of what helps individuals continue to develop and feel good about themselves. Having our lives organized in such a way as to be dependent on someone reminding us of obligations puts us in a kind of child position relating to a parent. How do people characterize someone who needs reminding regularly? Usually, as inadequate, not mature, not in control of his or her life, being the child in need of a parent. These are the cues that come through to the one being reminded.

However intense the cues, they serve their purpose, with the accumulation of other messages from the biological and sociological spheres, to help undermine feelings of confidence and self-esteem. Forgetting is common to all ages. Intervention processes focus on coping rather than catastrophizing about it. Keeping pen and paper handy for writing down things to be remembered can be helpful. Taping reminders on mirrors will help.

Before a care-giver decides to embark on a program of intervention, it is best to discuss the general direction with the older person. One such approach was tried with a 69-year-old female resident of a nursing home.

> Mrs. Jones had insisted that she could not walk to the dining room for her meals with all the other residents. No one raised much objection to bringing her trays to her room until one particular day while everyone was usually at supper, one of the staff noticed Mrs. Jones scurrying down the long hallway toward her room. She had been to the mailroom to see if a letter that she was very concerned about had arrived. She was having no problem walking. The staff decided, after a more thorough investigation and physical exam, that Mrs. Jones was able to walk to her meals in the dining hall. They decided to talk to her about their feelings that she was able to walk to the meals and that they did not want to take away any of her confidence by treating her as inadequate. They told Mrs. Jones that they would enjoy having her eat with the other residents, that she is so friendly that she can contribute a lot of encouragement to other residents. "We feel you can handle the walk to the dining room. We will be expecting you for dinner at 6:00 P.M. Would you like to walk down to the dining room now and pick out your table?"
>
> Mrs. Jones was rather taken back by the whole development and responded to the whole session by randomly telling the staff person, "No, I cannot walk that well." When the staff person did not respond to her protests about not being able to walk, Mrs. Jones began to sulk. She did not show up for dinner. Then the staff person began to get anxious. "It isn't working," she said to her colleagues. But, she decided to hang on for a while. Later that evening she made her routine rounds on the hall stopping by Mrs. Jones' room as usual. Mrs. Jones "chewed out" the staff person, accused her of not caring if she starved and threatened to leave the home. The staff person managed to keep herself from getting into a struggle with Mrs. Jones by saying only, "We missed you at supper," and then leaving the room. She was ready to scrap the whole approach until she saw wrappers from the snack machine in the trash can as she walked out the door. Mrs. Jones had walked down to the

snack machine during supper. It was not the most nutritious food but it did mean she was getting something. So it was decided to hold out a little longer. She did not come to breakfast, and no contact was made during the morning. About 15 minutes before lunch, Mrs. Jones appeared in the dining room. The staff person greeted everyone as usual and did the same to Mrs. Jones trying not to single her out. Mrs. Jones was noncommunicative to her greeting, but she was receiving so many welcomes from her friends that the rejection did not matter a lot. Mrs. Jones had made a tough decision when the unproductive behavior was no longer reinforced. She was still growing and was more independent today than she was yesterday, largely because the staff changed the feedback. Mrs. Jones was then more inclined to change her behavior.

Instead of reminding or doing *for* the older person what they could do for themselves, we recommend communicating something that says, "I believe you can handle it." This needs to be said in a supportive tone that reflects the inner feeling of "believing in" the person. When this is said to the older person, be prepared for a power struggle. Every resource available will be called upon to get you to continue feedback that reinforces their avoidance. Several techniques for getting out of a power struggle are available. If possible, try to ignore the onslaught. If ignoring is not applicable, remove yourself from the scene. At a later time, when the struggle has diminished, the situation can be discussed in a more rational context.

When responsibility is given to an older person and accepted, it is important that we do not attempt to take back the responsibility later.

Mrs. Flanders, 77 years old, had been encouraged to live with her married daughter, Peggy. Peggy wanted to give her mother a feeling of contributing in the family. She asked her mother if she would be willing to fix the evening meal during the week. Peggy, a writer, with an office at home, was relieved to have more time for her work, and her mother felt good about being able to give something to the family. On the first afternoon, Mrs. Flanders was busy in the kitchen getting supper ready. Peggy first heard a crash then something break. She hurried out of her office, found flour all over the kitchen floor and a broken glass in tiny pieces on the floor.

Peggy, an oldest child herself, told her mother, "Getting supper is just a chore and it is too much trouble for you. Why don't you go sit down at the TV in the living room and let me clean up this mess and finish supper?"

The temptation is great to take over responsibility that we give to older persons when they do not perform as efficiently as we would like. Intervention in the system will require staying out of responsibilities once they have been given. The cost of 25 pounds of spilled flour or a dozen broken glasses does not seem worth the price of reinforced dependency and lost courage.

Another intervention process involves a concerted effort to give older persons choices in as many areas of their lives as possible. "Do you want a half sandwich or a whole sandwich for lunch?" "Would you like to go shopping at 9:00 A.M. or 2:00 P.M.?" "Would you rather straighten your room before breakfast or after?" Making decisions is reinforcing for independence. Giving choices is a method which allows the care-giver to set and control the options offered, if that is necessary, but allows the older person to choose within those bounds.

Close kin to having choices is allowing older persons to participate in making the rules where they reside. Some rules may be nonnegotiable, such as the number of people who may occupy the room or how many people can be hired for the nutrition program of what constitutes personal embarrassment. But many rules can be democratically arrived at with respect to how a couple will divide up household chores, or how a nutrition program is to function, or how a nursing home is run. The encouraging care-giver will offer all opportunities possible to the elderly for participating in rule making. The leader might say something to the following effect:

> We, together, will be involved the next eight weeks in the special nutrition education program. It does not seem fair that I should make all the decisions. We can decide together how to decorate the rooms for the meetings, who the speakers will be for half the programs, how we want to structure the meeting time, and when and how long to have snack breaks and what to eat and drink. Who would like to work with a group to decorate? Who would like to . . .

It is so easy for those in charge to move in and take over programs, plan them, and get them done. Quite often we then wonder why it is that the elderly do not attend the meetings regularly or why they do not seem to appreciate all the work we do to organize and deliver a top-notch program. There is a fundamental law on human interaction: People tend to support those activities and programs for which they feel responsible.

If we encourage involvement and taking of responsibility, we should be prepared to let the chips fall. If the task succeeds, share the joy with those who participated. If a failure occurs, we do not need to feel sorry for those who worked hard but failed. Remember: "They can handle it." If we have a Mrs. Flanders who spills flour and breaks a glass or two, we need only allow her to handle the consequences of her work. If she does not know where the broom and dust scoop are stored, we could tell her where they are and get out of the situation quickly. Listening is very important but usually is more effective when everyone has calmed down and can more rationally discuss the matter.

We have suggested that some older persons, like some younger people for that matter, may engage in different levels of unproductive behavior in order to get the attention of others or control them. The reason for this is probably rooted in a deep-seated conviction that if other people had their "druthers," they would not choose to spend time with them. Another way of putting this is that most individuals do not feel that in and of themselves they are important to others. So they control—manipulate, if you will—others into situations designed to guarantee attention.

This interpretation of life was probably learned in early childhood. Most children learned early that if you behaved, you did not get too much attention. But if you misbehaved, you could guarantee that people would respond. Not in the most positive ways, but at least they would respond. Usually older married couples are quite skilled in these techniques. They still find that one partner only pays serious attention to the other if he or she is sick, or fusses, or complains.

One approach to intervening in this behavior involves a concerted effort to pay attention when it is not being asked for. Marital partners, family members, or friends can make good use of this emphasis. It serves to underline the notion that others *chose* to pay attention to them. They did not have to manipulate. The goal is to have them conclude: There must be something about me that is worthwhile. Most care-givers will be so relieved that the "manipulative" older individual is quietly involved or not fussing that they would not think of disturbing the calm. However, one way to lower the negative manipulative cycle for the long haul is to break the connection in the older person's head, "To get attention, to make sure you are considered, you have to manipulate." One long-term process involves entering the calm of the older person's life. This involves initiating attention when the older person is not asking for it. This behavior is saying, "You matter enough to me to choose to spend time with you."

INTERVENTION THROUGH RATIONAL RESTRUCTURING

The particular cognitive belief system held by older individuals will have decided influence upon how they interact with others in their social system. What the elderly believe about aging, about society's attitudes toward growing old can hinder their constructive behavior and guide the pattern that dependency responses will take in a social system.

From a rational restructuring perspective such as Ellis and Harper (1976) the assumption is that some elderly *allow* social attitudes to inhibit them. Social attitudes do not have power in and of themselves to hinder any elderly person from some measure of increased independent behavior. But how about social attitudes that result in fixed retirement at age 65? Doesn't that have the power to inhibit independence? Not necessarily. That attitude and social policy have only the power to stop an individual from regular employment at a full-time vocation. *That is all.* Even if it stopped a person from any kind of *employment*, social policy has no power to stop him from continued independent living and growth. That is a choice that remains with the older person. He or she can decide. He can upset himself by allowing mandatory retirement to affect him in all areas of life, but it is important to realize that the elderly person permitted it to affect him. He was in control and, in fact, still is. This realization is important for the elderly individual and for the professional. It establishes a point of contact, a reference point from which new strides toward individual integrity and responsibility can proceed.

Older individuals who are in poor health may not be able to achieve *levels* of independence that would be possible given a better physical condition. But, even in poor health, as in the cruel and inhuman Nazi concentration camps of Frankl's experience, there is one last element of independence that cannot be taken away from the aging individual: the independence to *choose how he will respond to poor health and the physical limitations of aging.* He can choose to feel sorry for himself, to allow it to make him more manipulative, to embitter him, even to break him. Or he can choose to respond in a more realistic manner: It would be nice if my health were better; I would rather it be different, but the world does not come to an end just because of ill health and *I can handle my responses to it.* I can choose not to upset myself with it. I can choose to respond in ways that reflect respect for myself and for others.

This approach to aging is fundamentally different from the "think positive" position many mistake it for. The "think positive" approach attempts to repress the reality of aging difficulties by forcing positive thoughts into the foreground of the conscious mind. The "think positive" attitude, while having some good points, in essence attempts to deny the fact of the problem. This seldom works. The approach here is to face the handicap squarely. The aging individual is helped to realize that it is his or her assumptions (attitudes) about ill health (or whatever is seen as the problem) that are causing the greatest amount of difficulty. These attitudes, common to so many, are expressed typically in one or more of the following ways: It is *awful* to be old; it is *terrible* to be old and ill at the same time; I *should not* have to experience life in this manner; if such a terrible thing happens to me, life is not worth living. Ellis and Harper argue that it is these assumptions that create depression, anger, anxiety, resentment, and so on. According to their position, neither age nor ill health has the power to produce such negative emotions as anger and resentment. It is, rather, our *assumptions about age and ill health* that have the power to create such emotions. So the intervention task is to replace the irrational assumptions with more rational ones. If irrational assumptions have the power to produce negative feelings, then rational assumptions will have the power to produce more positive emotions. It is irrational to conclude that it is awful to be old. "Awful," "terrible," imply unmanageability. It is an exercise in catastrophizing. It assumes an inherent power in aging, ill health, and so on that cannot be matched. Where is the evidence that establishes aging as awful or terrible? To conclude, "I should not have to experience aging/ill health" implies that the normal change process from time immemorial that results in decreases in adaptability and vulnerability to disease should be contravened for me. This is a most irrational conclusion, to say nothing of its implied grandiosity, to be repeating to oneself. It is, however, very common. In reality, if one were given to speaking in "shoulds," it would be more rational to conclude that everything has developed in such a way over time that aging and ill health should be occurring eventually to everyone.

The therapeutic task for the elderly person is really quite simple, but requires much practice: One should systematically and consistently *replace* the irrational assumptions with more rational ones, which in this case might be: *I wish it could have been avoided. I would rather it not have happened, but I can handle it. All the preparation over time has culminated just the way it should have: I should be aging and the coalescence of my bodily conditions could not have resulted in anything else but the illness. What can I do now to cope with the situation?* These new, more rational assumptions must be doggedly spoken to oneself at the time one upsets oneself with the lingering irrational beliefs and even when the elderly person anticipates their onset. Completely aware of the difficulty, the individual is helped to realize some fundamental realities: that the handicap does not nor cannot control him *unless he allows it to do so*; that the individual is in charge of his responses. At this point positive imaging can be of value. The elderly person closes his eyes and pictures himself replacing the irrational assumptions with more rational ones. He is to picture himself saying the more rational assumptions to himself and experiencing the positive feelings that result from the rational statements.

It should be obvious then how important to the aging person and professional is the relationship between biological decline and the accompanying attitudes. The biological decline is to be faced openly. Enough physiological knowledge is needed to determine the potential for actual physical development that is available as options for the elderly person for continued independence and enough knowledge to determine how much of his physical condition is psychogenic in origin. This approach has some research to support its effectiveness (Keller, Brooking, & Croake, 1975).

STRUCTURED REMINISCENCE AS INTERVENTION

When the care-giver takes the initiative and involves himself or herself with an older person the question of what to do or say that will be more helpful or growth-producing often comes up. A brand new structure on a very old practice is emerging as uniquely therapeutic for many old people. It is none other than the use of reminiscence as a counseling strategy.

The use of the term *reminiscence* in this context is simply defined as the calling to mind of an experience or fact from the past. Reminiscence has been shown to be an active attribute of all age groups, but is especially important and common during the later years (Lieberman & Falk, 1971). It may be viewed as a method whereby a person reflects upon past experiences, both positive and negative, in order to reconstruct and find additional significance and meaning. Buhler (1935) viewed reminiscence an inevitable part of the aging process. Her conclusion was that declines in accomplishments and abilities will result in a person's regression to the past in order to substantiate the worth of one's life. Neugarten (1964, p. 303) has viewed reminiscence as a part of human development during the later years:

> It is at this point in the life line that introspective increases and contemplation of one's inner thoughts becomes a characteristic form of mental life. The implication is not that the introspection of middle age is the same as the reminiscence of old age, but its forerunner. It is probably a preparatory step in the final structuring of the ego . . . the symbolic putting of one's house in order before one dies.

During recent years, renewed interest in reminiscence appeared to be "sparked" by Butler's (1963) article that proposed reminiscence to be a universal process that occurs in all older people. For Butler, the "life review" is a *conscious* and *purposeful* return to past experiences and conflict. This life review may be hurried along by biological, personal, and environmental circumstances. Butler made no attempt to speculate on the outcome of a life review, although he did indicate that the results could be either very positive or could "sculpture terrifying hatred out of fluid fitful antagonisms" (p. 408). Very positive effects of the life review have been supported by Lewis (1971), who provided evidence that this process of reminiscence may act to support the self-concept in times of pervasive stress.

Havighurst and Glasser (1972) attempted to describe the time devoted to, the nature of, and the quality of reminiscence in elderly subjects 62 years of age and over. Their conclusion was that there is an association between frequency of reminiscence, positive effects of the reminiscence, and personal-social adjustments, although no conclusion was reached as to which of the factors were causative and which were resultant.

The adaptive value of reminiscence was studied by McMahon and Rhudick (1967) through the use of nondirective interviews that attempted to assess the effects of depression and degree of intellectual decline or deterioration. High correlation was found between the frequency of reminiscence and freedom from depression as well as survival in a follow-up study performed one year later. Low correlation was noted between frequency of reminiscence and intellectual deterioration. McMahon and Rhudick concluded that reminiscence does, in fact, contribute to successful adaptation to life and old age in an achievement-oriented society.

Various indices to study four areas of reminiscence were developed by Lieberman and Falk (1971): (1) the importance of reminiscence to aged persons; (2) the restructuring of memories; (3) the selection process used by the individual in reporting his or her life history; and, (4) the role of particular recollections in the individual's current psychological economy. Data from this research revealed that the aged were considerably more interested in reminiscence activity than were the middle-aged. For the middle-aged, reminiscence functioned in the service of problem solving, whereas the elderly found reminiscence to mean far more in the area of personal satisfaction.

Coleman (1974) attributed three major functions to the reminiscence process: to bring forth and display a variety of interesting experiences that could be shared with a listener or reviewed with personal satisfaction; to bring some cognitive and emotional clarification to the life experience, as in the life review; and to show that the past has positive characteristics that would put present life, with all its negative stresses, in a more favorable light. Recent research by Hughston (1976) found reminiscence to be associated with increases in thinking abilities, with women showing more gain than men.

Although research support for extensive programs using past memories is relatively scant, evidence does suggest possibilities exist for effective use of reminiscence as an intervention technique with the aged. Individuals who work with the elderly may find reminiscence programs are effective in accomplishing the following objectives:

1. Elderly people may enjoy "getting back to things"; they may feel engaged and honored by another person's interest in their past experiences.

2. Reflection upon the past may serve to stimulate interest in present activities. Questions involving the way things are done today in comparison with the way things were done in the past can create interest in present activities.
3. Additional life meaning can be found in reflection upon past accomplishments as well as failures. Traumatic past experiences that have not been adequately dealt with should be avoided.
4. If reminiscence is an inevitable part of the aging process, it should be used to the fullest extent possible in order to create worth and value of past life experiences.
5. Reminiscence can benefit social development, in that it can serve to stimulate common bonds, experiences, and beliefs. For example, simply reflecting upon the Great Depression will stimulate a large amount of interest among those cohorts who went through the depression together. The same thing would be true with those experiencing other historical events such as World War I and II.

Reminiscence may be used in order to stimulate thinking processes in elderly people (Hughston, 1976). It appears to be a well-recognized fact that aged individuals enjoy spending time thinking and discussing things that happened many years ago. This reflection upon the past may provide material that has great individual meaning as it brings to mind many very special experiences that happened years ago. If interest is shown in things an elderly person has done during their earlier life, rapport may be more easily established, mutual interests may develop, and, most important, the mind may start to exercise itself. Reminiscence can serve as a "hooking" mechanism whereby an aged person is enticed into areas of interest that have not been reflected upon for many years. It has also been noted by Hughston that old people who were previously not interested in cooperating with present-oriented projects appear to be much more cooperative when their interest is stimulated with long-ago events or happenings.

It is valuable to use reminiscence programs that are designed to require as much cognitive activity as possible. Examples of successful reminiscence activities are given in the Appendix. These are not presented as being applicable to all elderly people but should be viewed as examples of activities that have been found to be effective with some aged individuals.

Each activity involves a small amount of writing and scoring. Although this is not completely mandatory, recording of work and scores provides a measure whereby the counselor may judge improvement as well as keep a record of the amount of reminiscence work done. Packets of reminiscence materials may also be provided in order to allow self-reminiscence or enrichment experiences to be completed at the elderly person's leisure. The development of the packets could function in almost the same manner as a crossword puzzle.

USE OF CONTRACTS IN INTERVENTION

For various conflicts a behavior contract can be an effective strategy for promoting desirable behavior and extinguishing undesirable patterns. The consequences of the undesirable behavior are specifically prescribed and are to be decided upon in mutual agreement with all parties involved. The consequences for the desirable behavior are defined and agreed upon. The responsibilities and expectations of all parties to the contract are clearly specified. It is important to be so clear that nothing is left to individual interpretation.

Being insistent on specificity will pay off in accomplishing the contractual goals. Failures to keep the contract can be quickly and easily determined. Changes can be easily made for ineffective or inappropriate elements of the contract.

There are a few specific guidelines for structuring contracts. First, the problem must be defined specifically, so specifically that one would have no question as to whether the behavior occurred and could easily count the number of times the behavior did occur. "She is uncooperative" is not adequate as a definition. *How* is she uncooperative? Does she refuse to carry out agreed-upon responsibilities with her room or her household duties? Is the uncooperativeness related to habits of personal cleanliness or to discourteous ways of relating to others? "Refused to carry plate and silverware back to the kitchen" is specific enough for contracting purposes.

Second, the new desirable behavior for the older person needs to be decided just as specifically and agreed upon by everyone involved. If the elderly individual is not bringing the plate and silverware back to the kitchen, did she have a chance to participate in deciding that chore? Are there any other extenuating circumstances?

When it appears that a problem has been isolated and defined specifically, it is very important to observe the individual's behavior for a specified amount of time. These observations usually take place before any helping strategy is applied.

The significance of observation procedures has not always been clearly recognized. Some may object to using this technique because it appears to be unnecessary and/or it is perceived as too much trouble. Others view the procedure as mechanical, cold, and unrelated to the treatment process.

Accurate and careful observation of an elderly individual's behavior prior to any treatment is essential for sorting fact from fiction.

It may *seem*, for example, that Mrs. Jones *never* brings her plate and silverware into the kitchen. Observations can clarify exaggerated interpretations of behavior of older persons.

Behavior observations can also be used after a treatment process has begun for giving objective feedback about the effectiveness of the technique(s) being used. This is the most accurate check available as to whether the suggested treatment should be continued, altered, or discontinued. Further objective records can serve as effective reinforcers that clearly demonstrate the small and continuous changes in the behavior of the older person.

Types of Observations

There are basically two types of observations that most behaviorists make use of in natural settings of older individuals. Type one is called a "frequency count." It is the number of times a particular behavior is exhibited. A "frequency count" might be taken of Mrs. Jones and her plate and silverware. The number of times she carries them to the kitchen daily represents a "frequency count." This procedure can be applied to most behaviors.

Type two observational method is the "time interval." The *length* of time an undesirable behavior is exhibited is recorded. If the nature of the problem behavior is not frequency but duration, then "time interval" is used. "Pouting" might be best observed by how long the behavior occurs, rather than how frequent. The frequency of pouting may not be excessive, but the duration of each pouting episode may indicate a problem. In most natural settings of older individuals the "frequency count" method is more useful than the "time interval."

Procedures for Observing Behavior

1. Define specifically the behavior to be observed. Frequently, the behavior to be changed and the process for coping with it are worded in vague descriptions, such as "Mr. Jones is a negative person." "Mrs. Jones needs to become more independent" is also too general. "Mr. Jones curses and swears when he is denied a request" is a specific description that can be easily counted. "Mrs. Jones needs to get ready herself and be on time for the daily nutrition pickup at her house at 9:30 A.M." is specific and measurable independence.
2. The setting in which the behavior will be observed needs to be determined. Suppose Mr. Jones uses profanity at the senior citizens' center. Let's say we also know from his wife that he uses profanity in the privacy of his home, and when he and a

friend are off talking together by themselves. If it is decided to modify the swearing in public, observations would be carried out only in these public settings and not in his home or when he is off talking with a friend.

3. Usually one behavior at a time is measured. In this case an *A* might be used to indicate the performance of the behavior during a specific time interval, and a *B* if it does not occur.
4. Normally a full week is used for observing behavior. Longer periods may be used if necessary. Usually the behavior in question will be observed for a 45-minute to one-hour period. The patterns of the older person and the behavior to be observed will determine when during the day this period will occur. Mr. Jones's swearing in public will need to be observed during that interval in the daily schedule that involves public interaction between himself and other individuals. With some types of behavior a modified interval is suggested. This involves distributing the 45-minute period throughout the day. This procedure is useful when a particular encouraging technique has been initiated with an older person and the goal is to find out whether it is successful.
5. The behavior is recorded and marked on a graph. The graph reveals a pattern of responses that is easily and quickly interpreted. For example, on the first day of observation Mrs. Jones took her plate and silverware to the kitchen once. The second and third day she refused to take them back at all. Then on the fourth and fifth days they were removed once each day. After a particular encouragement strategy has been initiated with Mrs. Jones, her progress from the original behavior frequency can again be charted.

Contract Process

To initiate a behavior contract an agreement between two or more parties is needed. The agreement is to fulfill certain specified and agreed-upon behavior, expectations, and responsibilities. Each person's role should be clearly spelled out so that there can be no disagreement about infractions. Positive consequences and negative consequences are spelled out. They are dependent upon the behavior chosen by the older individual.

Contracts usually involve two types: individual and exchange. Individual contracts are useful to help an individual increase a desired behavior that does not affect another person. For example, an individual contract is often used with undesirable habits an older person might like to discontinue. On the other hand, exchange contracts involve two or more parties. One of the advantages of contracts is that they do not have to have a professional to initiate them. Exchange contracts can be worked out between spouses, relatives or friends on their own. For more details on self-help marriage contracts the reader should see Knox's (1975) *Marital Exercise Book.*

An individual contract with Mr. Fred Bowles (fictitious) was established to help him cope with the problem of loss of control of his temper. Specifically defined, the behavior was listed as: shouting, blaming, and slamming doors. The undesirable behavior was observed for a week and charted. The desired new behavior was agreed upon by the older person. It included speaking in normal voice tones, presenting his concerns at the weekly group council (discussed in Chapter 7) meeting, and closing his door softly.

A list of favorite activities and treats that Mr. Bowles enjoys daily and weekly was drawn up. There are several ways to obtain such a list. By observing what the older person likes to do, a list of positive consequences can be collected. If this is not feasible, a more direct approach can be used. Mr. Bowles was asked what things he really enjoyed doing that occurred daily. These activities and treats were rank-ordered, with the most favorite placed at the top of the list.

It is very important that the discussion of the contract take place at a time mutually agreeable to all parties and *not* near the time of the display of undesirable behavior. The setting should be pleasant and the emotional level calm for a clear and succinct discussion of the contract.

Agreement then is ready to be reached with respect to which positive consequence is to accompany the successful performance of the new behavior and which negative consequence is to occur if the new behavior does not occur. It is usually better to have the consequence be as logically related to the behaviors as possible. In some cases this may not be feasible. Once this agreement is reached the contract is complete.

Another example involved Mrs. Grave, who left her door open regularly while watching TV. Because the noise disturbed others in the family, it was agreed that anyone who chose to watch TV in his or her room (including grandmother, parents, and children) would close their doors. The contract was drawn up with Mrs. Grave's agreement along with all family members. Negative consequences were spelled out, along with privileges. Approaching the behavior problem in this direct, yet democratic manner, Mrs. Grave was able to decide to cooperate.

Mr. Jackson, age 77, was living with his daughter's family at their home. The daughter was perplexed as to what to do about her father's pattern of spending his personal allowance at the first of every month. They had agreed that $30 of his monthly retirement checks would be his personal allowance. The rest was used for food, medicine, and clothes. The personal allowance was to be used for entertainment, personal items like razor blades, shaving lotion, and any "extras" he could buy with what was left. For several months he had spent all his allowance in the first week of the month and came back to his daughter for more money. Even though he was spending all his allowance before the middle of the month, Mr. Jackson was outspoken about getting all of the $30 at the first of the month. A contract was suggested.

Mr. and Mrs. Ewing, he 70, she 68, complained about conflict since he had retired. She felt that he could help around the house more since he was retired. She indicated that she had to do all the vacuuming, dusting, straightening, and cooking. He read his paper, fished, and spent time with the "boys," she said. He said she accused him of getting in the way when he tried to help, and, also, he was angry because she was not willing to have sexual intercourse anymore. An exchange contract was suggested.

Exchange Contract

An example of an exchange contract is as follows:

> In order to improve our marriage and our feelings for each other, Mr. Ewing agrees to vacuum the house twice a week (Wednesday and Saturday) and dust on Saturday if, in return, Mrs. Ewing agrees to participate in sexual intercourse at least once a week. The terms of this contract are fixed for one week only. After one week, this contract may be extended or a new contract negotiated. We further agree to keep a record of our own agreed-upon behavior and our partner's for one week.
>
> Signed: ______________ Mrs. Ewing
> ______________ Mr. Ewing
> ______________ Care-giver
>
> Date______

Several assumptions underpin contracting as a process for bringing change to individual's lives. First, it is assumed that behavior is "learned." Whatever particular behavior an individual acts out is the result of having been "learned." When an older person says "I am anxious all the time," or "Life is not enjoyable," the first task of the care-giver is to discover what specific behavioral actions (including expectations, words) are behind the expressed feelings. When these negative actions are changed, the probability increases for the presence of satisfactory feelings in the elderly individual.

A second assumption underlying the contract approach is that attitudes and feelings have their origin in behavior. The older person may be anxious because in her relationship with her daughter there have been no clear rules and expectations formulated with regard to responsibilities and privileges. The older individual often discovers what responsibilities were expected of him *after* he or she has failed to fulfill unspoken desires. Little discussion usually takes place with regard to individual's expectations of others. When the current pattern of behavior is changed and expectations are cleared *beforehand*, the probability is high that the older person's anxiety will be lowered. This is the foundation for the third assumption, which is, behavior can be changed! If expectations are carefully *stated ahead*, anticipated responsibilities, consequences, and desirable behavior can be increased and undesirable responses lessened.

The popular belief that individuals must change their attitude before they can change their actions is not held by most behavioral counselors. The evidence, behavioralists believe, is that behavior can be changed first, and in most cases it is much easier and more effective. When behavior that irritates is changed, immediately the negative impact on another person's feelings has ceased, and thus new feedback is possible in the system. If the irritating behavior is replaced by behavior that communicates satisfying feelings to another person, the process of behavior change *has begun*. Individuals cannot build relationships on irritating responses. If we wait for behavior to change until the individual "feels" like changing, we have no structural support for nudging the feelings toward a positive expression. This is especially true if we expect the cooperative attitude to change *in the presence of irritating behavior*. The probability is much higher that attitudes and feelings will *follow along* if behavior changes.

NEED FOR ASSERTIVE BEHAVIOR

For older persons whose behavior in social systems is hampered by conflicts between themselves and others, contracts are helpful. However, for many elderly, independence needs are hindered by a lack of social skills for asserting themselves. They may be either too passive or aggressive in their response patterns with others.

Elderly individuals are frequently heard expressing strong feelings of having very little influence on matters that really count. There is a structure available today for enabling individuals to overcome their feelings of personal lack or control over their life. We cannot simply go on blaming our condition upon the modern technological world filled with power brokers who exploit individuals. The development of our interpretations of the world and how to survive in it came about as survival strategies we learned in early childhood. We cannot be responsible for the surrounding into which we were born or for the people who either encouraged or discouraged our independence in the early years. We did not choose the family into which we would be born, nor did we choose the method of nurturance. We formed certain conclusions about life and the world and how to relate to others in the world. We cannot change our past. But we can change our interpretations about our past. Further, if we *continue today to operate out of the contexts of our early intepretations, it is our choice.* We have no basis now to blame parents, early conditioning, society, or government. We have choices each day about how we will act in a multitude of situations.

Assertive development as an intervention strategy is a concern for elderly to recognize so that they can begin to cope with the problem of nonassertiveness in everyday living: in homes, stores, restaurants, club meetings, supermarkets, nursing homes, or wherever their daily routines bring them. Situations daily confront each of us that leave us shaken, anxious, frustrated, and angry; for example, our personal needs are not listened to because, being elderly, we are "supposed" to be grouchy; we are treated like a child and made to feel inadequate and dependent; someone who has not paid back already borrowed money now asks us for more; someone cuts in front of us in line; a salesman is so persuasive that we bought something we did not want; we were deliberately overcharged for house repairs; we do not feel comfortable beginning conversation with strangers at a meeting; we feel unable to express caring feelings to another person; and so on.

Individuals, especially the elderly, need to learn ways to act in their own best interests. They need to be able to stand up for themselves comfortably, to speak out for their own rights without limiting the rights of others in the process. This is what is meant by assertiveness. According to Alberti and Emmons (1974), lack of assertiveness is generally expressed in one of two ways. If we consider assertiveness as the center of a line, to the left of center we might describe one of the ways of behaving as submissive, "super-nice," self-effacing. On the right side of the assertiveness position we would list the second way of behaving that shows lack of assertiveness as "aggressive."

Passive   Assertive   Aggressive

Most individuals have difficulty knowing how to distinguish between assertive and aggressive behavior. Passive action is more easily identified, but its negative effects are not so clearly understood.

Individuals whose life-style is characterized primarily by passive behavior are generally more dishonest in their feelings and more cautious in their behavior. The actual internal reactions from nonassertive passive responses are feelings of hurt, uneasiness, or uncomfortableness at the time of the transaction, and a feeling of anger later. It is not just a coincidence that the male finds anger feelings welling up while he is shaving, the female while curling her hair. It is to the mirror that we direct our angry comments that we wished we had spoken at the time the incident occurred. It is the caution, the guarded stance of the passive individual that serves to actually keep the angry feelings from being felt at the time of the actual incident. They seep out later through layers of defensive caution.

To the surprise of many, other people do not usually respond favorably to "mister nice guy." They may actually be irritated at the passive reaction or even incited to more aggressive behavior. It is not unusual to find aggressive individuals increase their offensiveness in order to provoke the passive individual into responding more as a human being instead of as a doormat.

We have received a lot of training for the passive role, particularly women and older persons in general. From the earliest years females have been nurtured to play passive roles. Religious teachings have encouraged individuals to deny themselves. From our family and from society we have also learned how to aggressively control others and circumstances.

Being assertive is not the same thing as being aggressive, nor does it mean being a patsy. Aggressive responses may very well involve honest expressions of feelings, but the aggressive reaction is at the expense of another person. It is honesty of the overkill variety, which comes off to others as righteous, superior, and/or as a put-down. The overly expressive response causes anger, resentment, and a desire by the other person to get even. Aggressive behavior enhances the self but must put down another in the process. To act assertively an individual does not have to hurt others or deny their rights in the process. Assertive actions are more aboveboard and flexible, and they reflect awareness of the rights of others while securing one's own rights. Although the aggressive individual usually overreacts, making an indelible impression he or she may later regret, the passive individual so underreacts that if an appropriate response comes, it will be *after* the interaction has been closed.

Anxiety is one of the chief psychological problems of the elderly, so the research indicates. Experience and empirical investigations with assertiveness indicate that if individuals act assertively where they had previously responded passively or aggressively, they will find their anxiety lowered from those situations (Keller, Brooking, & Croake, 1975). Stand up for your rights and you reduce tension *and* increase your sense of worth as a person.

Many elderly individuals have gone through life under the impression that they were under *obligation*, almost, to give in to the wishes of others. This was encouraged with the unfortunate notion that parents were supposed to deny their own rights and give in to all wishes of their children. Children's interests were not to be denied, ever. This was the criteria for many as to whether or not they were good parents. They were not to think of their own rights. Good parents did not dwell on their wishes. Parents seemed to fear even the appearance of concern for themselves. But what was the result of this stance? Disappointment and anger raged among parents. After all they had sacrificed and denied, there were few appreciative children! In fact, the more parents denied their own self-respect the more disrespect the children showed. Parents failed to see the simple connection: Children did not give respect because parents did not respect themselves. This is what assertiveness is all about. The elderly can encourage respect from others by respecting themselves more. Always giving into the wishes of others, sitting on your own interests, or cutting others down in order to get your way diminishes feelings of personal worth.

There is a kind of romantic expectation that lingers in many: If others "cared," they would not only "know" what our interests were but they would see to it that our rights are preserved. Even though this belief does not, never has, and never will work, it runs deep among many older persons. If our rights are to be respected, it is *our* responsibility to speak up. If our interests are to be taken seriously, it is up to *us* to communicate those desires.

When older persons behave assertively, they actually are modifying their environment in a way that usually brings them better feelings, more satisfying relationships, and stronger self-concept from more positive feedback. Ego strength is not a commodity that we inherit, nor it is something mystical and spooky that only the "groovy" people experience. Ego strength is a result of all the ways we operate in the world. It comes from doing things that give feedback that says, "You are OK." No matter how old the individual, positive feedback will result in better ego strength, less manipulative dependency, and greater potential for preserving independence.

GUIDELINES FOR CHOOSING LEVEL OF INTERVENTION

The care-giver working with older individuals in more direct counseling contexts faces daily the dilemma of how to intervene in social situations that are never the same. Should the behavior be ignored, a contract drawn up, assertiveness taught, or is participating in the drawing up of rules perhaps the appropriate strategy? A basic rule of counseling intervention with the elderly is to have a medical examination to check for possible organic sources of behavioral dysfunction. Further, it is important to check for information in order to rule out problems involving nutrition, adequacy of financial income, residence, and transportation. This needs to be accomplished before making decisions about what particular counseling strategy to apply or what level of unproductive behavior may be at work (Chapter 3). This approach assumes that we have an older person who is in reasonably good physical health (absence of paralysis, brain damage, or serious pathology from chemical imbalance) and whose basic life needs are accounted for.

Level One

Unproductive behavior at this level is described as "Attention-gaining." The purpose of the older person's behavior can be determined by the care-giver monitoring his or her *own* internal feelings. If the care-giver feels somewhat annoyed, but no more, or if the behavior tempts his or her to want to "remind," it can be reasonably assumed that the *goal* of the elderly individual is getting attention.

What could be behind this type of behavior is a feeling of uneasiness about whether the older person really belongs, whether he has a place, whether he is really valued if he is not the center of attention. This patterned behavior can be annoying. If the object of the attention (partner, friend, etc.) tries to stop this behavior by a *corrective* response that demands, orders, or shames, the older person may stop the unproductive behavior, temporarily, when attention is received. He has achieved his feedback goal, but the unfortunate cycle is reinforced. Manipulation and all the bad feelings from negative responses are bedfellows of this attention. If you are fairly sure the older person is at level one, then proceed with appropriate strategies at this level. An intervention procedure that just "ignores" the unhealthy attention seeking will not be effective in the long run. It must be accompanied by a second procedure that involves initiating or scheduling attention when the older person is not seeking it. This is a basic pattern that should be put into operation before—and even alongside—any other strategies.

Making use of encouraging words, schedules, and processes represents another broad-based attack on the attention-getting behavior. This approach involves a structural attempt for conveying respect and encouragement to older persons. The nature of manipulative processes to gain attention using overly passive or aggressive behavior may indicate the appropriateness of assertive training for older persons at this level.

Level Two

The general characteristic of unproductive behavior at level two is "Bossy." Care-givers can check out their suspicions by evaluating their own internal feelings. If those messages seem to be communicating to the care-giver feelings of a need to reassert control, it can be reliably assumed that the goal of the older person's behavior is the same: to establish control. The care-giver's feelings toward the older person may be something like "you can't get away with that." The care-giver's own internal responses are strong clues about what is the purpose of the older person's behavior in the social system.

When the elderly person is engaged primarily in bossy-type behavior, it can be assumed that he is feeling that he has no place unless he is in control, or that he counts for something only when he keeps others busy with him. These are hidden feelings of inadequacy that are compensated for by using most situations as opportunities to prove he is worthwhile by taking charge of people and situations either directly or indirectly.

If the care-giver responds to these controlling responses with feedback that is corrective or "checkmate" in nature, the older individual responds by intensifying his action by either acting more aggressively or by becoming even more uncooperative. Therefore, one appropriate basic strategy for the care-giver with older individuals at level two is self-removal from the conflict. This can be done in many different ways. The care-giver might choose to introduce his leaving by saying "I would be willing to talk with you about this at another time. Right now does not seem to me to be the best for objectively resolving the problem." Then *leave*! If the same situation occurs again later, the care-giver need not say anything. Just leave! This action implies self-respect, and it does not reinforce the manipulative bossy behavior. It is assumed that the care-giver has begun the process of initiating attention at nonmanipulative moments and that encouragement processes are in progress.

At this level contracting is quite useful (see the contracting discussion in this chapter for examples). The aggressive actions associated with the bossy level also indicate the appropriateness of developing the social skill of assertiveness.

Level Three

Behaviorally, level 3 is characterized by "Counter-hurt, wherein older individuals say by their actions that they have been so hurt by others that they seek to hurt back. This often gets translated into the terms of the "martyr." "I have a place when I am hurt by others." There is, for these individuals, a kind of masochistic satisfaction in being hurt, and as a compensation for feelings of inadequacy, they nurture a feeling that they count for something when they hurt back.

Again, care-givers can usually tell whether the older individual is at this level by checking out their own internal feelings. If the care-giver feels angry, hurt, or has thoughts like "after all I have done for you, look what you did," it can be assumed that the purpose of the older person's behavior was to hurt. Some care-givers may have problems here. They may have so programmed themselves to deny any inner feelings of desire to hurt that they may not be enough in tune with their own responses to use this procedure.

If the care-giver reacts in a corrective way to try to stop the behavior, it intensifies the desire of the older person to get even. Then he or she will react in even more unattractive ways.

The strategies suggested for the care-giver assume the broad-based action of initiating time spent with the older person if at all possible. The care-giver will certainly want to avoid revengeful acts and may also choose to remove himself or herself from the "hurtful" scene and talk with the older person at a more "objective" time later.

Behavior at this level represents a more serious progression. For this reason care-givers will want to reevaluate the nature of their relationship with the older person. The communication of dignity and respect should be reviewed. Is the older person being treated as a dependent child? There may well be some serious breaches in respect for the older individual. Encouragement procedures are a basic requirement. Contracting is a valid process for dealing with behavior at this level. The "hurt" syndrome may indicate the appropriateness of rational restructuring and/or assertive training for older individuals at this level since somehow their own rights and desires are felt to be unmet.

Level Four

The most serious behavior, represented by level four, is described as "Disablement." The older person is communicating through his actions that the only way he feels he counts for something is to have people stop expecting anything of him. He is saying by his actions, "get off my back." The older person does not desire to be *totally* ignored, only to cease expecting any responsibility. This is a very discouraged older person. His behavior masks strong feelings of inadequacy. Failure is so feared that all willingness to risk is gone.

The care-giver looks for a clue as to whether the older individual is at this level by again checking his own internal reactions. If the care-giver feels anything like "I give up," or "I cannot do anything with this person," it can be assumed that the purpose of the older person's behavior was to get the care-giver to give up on him. If the care-giver uses corrective approaches to try to bring the older person around, he is met by *more* passive resistance. The older person withdraws even more.

Behavior at this level will demand more intense remedial strategies. Basic approaches of intervention, initiating interest in the older person, touching, are to be assumed. Informal contracts that offer tangible rewards for positive movement toward assuming responsibility are useful here. Encouragement strategies will probably be more effective after some movement occurs through the tangible reward informal contract. See Chapter 5 for case studies at each level.

SUMMARY

Older persons who are growing in their independence are to be encouraged. They are going to make it. Others will be motivated toward increased freedom by ceasing to fight with themselves and starting to take more responsibility for their own lives. Intervention approaches that communicate respect for older persons will be useful in most contexts. The value of reminiscence for intervention is just being discovered and has broad application possibilities. More structured approaches, such as assertive training and contracting, may be called for in certain situations. The approaches used will vary from individual to individual, but the overall goals focus on the individual in a social system with a view to circumventing reinforcement of avoidance behaviors and reinforcing the independence and growth of old people. Attitudes that foster increased participation of the elderly in decision making and in the direction of their own lives are basic to promotion of independence. The result of increased independence and confidence is often seen in the renewed interest in contributing to the life satisfaction of other elderly persons.

To promote motivation among elderly individuals a care-giver needs a wide range of resources and a basic reference point. An attitude that intuitively encourages the capability of the older person and a knowledge of many resources for supporting this notion has been presented in this chapter. This basic attitude and resources for reinforcing it were drawn together in a structure to provide guidance for interpreting different levels of unproductive behavior and appropriate remedial approaches. Case studies illustrating this approach are presented in Chapter 6. To be successful with these approaches implies a

Table 4–1 LEVELS OF UNPRODUCTIVE BEHAVIOR, REACTIONS, AND SUGGESTED INTERVENTION STRATEGIES

Implicit belief of older person carrying out unproductive behavior	Level[a]	How care-giving individual feels	Older person's reaction to corrective approach	Intervention suggestions
I have a place, I belong, when attention is focused on me. (Hidden feelings of inadequacy)	ATTENTION	Mildly annoyed, temptation to remind	May stop unproductive behavior temporarily when attention is received	Ignore unproductive attention seeking and initiate attention at pleasant times; use encouragement processes, assertive skills development; social involvement encouraged; rational restructuring
I have a place, when I am in control, I feel I count for something when I keep you "busy" with me. (Hidden feelings of inadequacy)	BOSSY	Provoked, feeling a need to reassert control, feeling that "you can't get away with that"	Intensifies the action when challenged	Remove self from conflict; schedule time; use contracting procedures; assertive development; relaxation procedures; encourage social involvement; rational restructuring

I have a place when I am hurt by others; I count for something when I can hurt others in return. (Hidden feelings of inadequacy)	COUNTER-HURT	Angry, hurt, and "after all I have done"	Intensifies desire to get even; acts in more unattractive ways	Avoid revenge; remove self from power struggle; reevaluate nature of relationship; schedule time; communication of dignity and respect; use contracting procedures; rational restructuring; assertive development; encourage social involvement
I count for something when people "get off my back." (Strong feelings of inadequacy)	DISABLEMENT	"I give up"; "I have had it up to here with this person"; "I cannot do anything with this person"; futile	No use to try; passive; withdraws	Reality therapy; milieu therapy; informal contracts with tangible rewards; when some progress occurs use democratic processes: faith in person, emphasis on respect and dignity

Chart developed by Rudolph Dreikurs and G. Hugh Allred. Revised by James F. Keller.

[a] Each level represents the purpose of the older individual's behavior. To determine the older person's level check your inner feelings and the response of the older person.

knowledge background and a holistic support structure. An awareness of distinctions between myth and reality in the current demographic trends is a must. Encouragement toward more independent behavior for the elderly assumes an awareness of the biological aging process and the difference between the aging condition and the potential available for development.

Chapter 5
Intervention in Specific Problems

The challenge of intervening in social systems is to enable older persons to experience increased development of potential and responsibility for their own lives. It is equally exciting to see their quality of life improve in the later years. In Chapter 4 the basic philosophy of this approach was described, primarily in theoretical terms. Now an attempt to capture this philosophy is made in terms of actual specific case studies. These will give you, the reader, an opportunity to try your wings by imagining yourself confronted by the situation described and thinking through your own responses.

From the many case studies collected over the years representative problems have been selected. These situations portray typical examples of unproductive behavior of older people that are likely to confront care-givers.

The situations presented reflect the typical range of ordinary garden-variety neuroses. This means that this book is primarily applicable to typical maladjustment problems that countless thousands live with daily. Chronic organic syndromes are not covered by the theory and strategies presented here. It is much more likely that the problems that plague the majority of older persons are not organic but psychogenic in nature. Some may see these problems as fairly "normal" behavior for older people and should just be "accepted." In many cases this point is certainly valid, and yet it is precisely problems at this level that have been most frequently presented as difficulties by nurses, social workers, nursing home staff, and other professionals who counsel the elderly.

One of the problems with most case study presentations is that not enough of the process is given for the reader to get a handle on the method. In order to deal with this shortcoming, the first case studies will be described in more detail.

A typical example of unproductive behavior will be presented. A standard format will follow under the *recommendation* section. The reader will be asked to seek the level that the unproductive behavior represents. Then specific suggestions for intervention will follow.

SITUATION 1: WILL NOT CHANGE CLOTHES

Mr. S is 88 years old, college educated, a widower, one of nine children. There were three girls, then Mr. S, then three more girls, then two boys. Prior to coming to the nursing home, Mr. S had lived in an apartment with one of his brothers. He now has a problem with a skin graft that had not healed properly. Several different treatments have been tried and the problem seems to be clearing up. He really looks forward to going into town on the nursing home bus twice a week.

The general problem with Mr. S had earlier revolved around his trying to tell the staff how they should carry out their work (something like he used to do with the five children in his family who were born after him). Lately, however, he has refused to change his clothes after bathing. Many residents have complained about his odors.

Resolution Process

• Determine the level of unproductive behavior. Being alert to how people in his social system respond to his behavior will help make this decision.

Mr. S seems to be concerned with power. The reactions of the staff have been focused around trying to make him change his clothes with a feeling of needing to show him that he must follow certain rules. This need to control Mr. S is good evidence that he is struggling with the staff to show them he does not have to follow their rules. He will show them that they cannot make him do what he does not wish to do. The feedback from the staff has served to reinforce

Mr. S's unproductive behavior. The fact that they tried to force him to comply encouraged him to resist.

- Reexamine the nature of the relationship of the staff to residents.

- Have staff relate to residents in more democratic styles.

- Draw up a contract with Mr. S. Identify the desirable behavior specifically: to put on clean clothes after each bath. Both the staff person and Mr. S agreed on two baths per week. Undesirable behavior is defined as putting on the same clothes after his bath that he wore prior to the bath.

- Since he really likes to ride the bus to town, the positive consequences to changing his clothes after each bath was suggested as being able to go to town. If he puts on the same clothes after his bath he loses the privilege of going to town once that week.

- Both the staff and Mr. S must agree on the positive and negative consequences. For this situation more detail about how the recommendations are to be carried out will be given. This will serve as a kind of model for the process of implementing the other case studies.

Intervening with a contract seemed appropriate. Working out the contract is best accomplished by a staff person who relates well to the individual. It should be done at a time other than when the bath is being taken. It is important that the staff person approach the contract discussion with a respectful nonaccusatory posture. It might begin by saying something like, "Mr. S, one of the things I want to avoid at our home is giving impressions that only the staff is capable of making the rules. We are all here together. We share at least eight hours a day, six days a week. That is a lot of time. I would like it better if we worked out needed rules together rather than my arbitrarily imposing them. Would you like to participate in making the rules that can be decided by all? . . . There is one problem I would like to discuss with you and have us work out together. Would it be all right with you if we discussed it now, or would you rather we set another time?" (With this approach there is almost always a readiness to discuss the problem then. If a joint decision is reached to postpone the discussion, a specific time for scheduling should be made. The respect communicated to the older person will pay off in more positive dividends than the lost time will hinder the situation.) "The problem has to do with putting on clean clothes after your bath. Perhaps, it would be best to agree on how many baths per week would be appropriate."

Suppose Mr. S says, "Once a week is enough." The staff person should avoid ridicule, shame, criticism, and argument that would encourage Mr. S's unproductive behavior.

Perhaps the staff member could say something like, "If you really feel like you should take only one bath a week, I guess you have a right to feel that way. I cannot force you to change your mind. How could we work it out so you can have the right to take a bath only once a week and others have the right to congregate at our meals and meetings without being disturbed by odors that may develop from seven days without a bath?" (This approach, grounded in respect, fair treatment for all, and democratic decision making, usually eliminates the need for unproductive behavior and *wins* cooperation. The reader should note that Mr. S has not been granted the freedom to do as he pleases. What is different is the approach.)

This style is so disarming that the individual usually responds with something like, "Well, how many times do you think I should bathe?"

In a case like this, where Mr. S has a strong bossy history, the care-giver would best avoid making suggestions. The Mr. S's of the world do not have enough history of being approached this way to trust it immediately. The care-giver might say, "I am not sure, how many would you be willing to take per week?" It was at this point Mr. S agreed to take two baths.

The staff person felt, since it was during the winter that this was reasonable to try, so he said, "Why don't we try two baths per week and see how it works out?" Mr. S agreed.

The way had been paved for a reasonable discussion of the more volatile issue of putting on clean clothes after each bath. The staff person began, "I feel we have a problem with putting back on the same clothes after bathing that you had on before. Since we drive into town on Monday and Friday afternoon, how would it be with you if you bathed and changed into clean clothes before each trip?" (The democratic respect-oriented approach usually encourages cooperation.) "Since we all will be sitting pretty close for the 30-minute ride, would it be acceptable with you to have the agreement that if you have your bath and clean clothes on that you have decided you wish to go into town with us? And, that if you do not have your bath or if you have had your bath but have not put on clean clothes, this means you have decided you do not wish to go into town with us?"

This approach to contract writing with older persons is much more likely to obtain their cooperation. After the general democratic respect-oriented approach becomes generally practiced the need for unproductive behavior declines as does the need for contracts.

SITUATION 2: DEPRESSION

Mr. H, age 72, was formerly a city engineer and is now retired, married, and living with his spouse in an apartment. His health is good and activity level has been high. Mr. H came in for counseling. He complained of continuing depression and loss of interest in activities. His physician had indicated that no organic problem was causing the depression.

Resolution Process

- Obtain as much information as possible about his depressed feelings. Mr. H indicated his wife had been in the hospital and had been home for about three weeks. His depression began about three weeks prior to his coming in for counseling. More details showed that Mr. H's two daughters, who live 500 miles away, had spent two of the three weeks with Mr. H and Mrs. H. They cooked the meals and took care of details of housekeeping. The daughters had gone home now and Mr. H's depression seemed worse. Mrs. H was still weak and Mr. H felt she needed rather constant care and observation.

- Due to the intensity of his depression, a greater amount of time was taken to display empathy and warmth to Mr. H so that he would be encouraged to talk more about it.

- Determine level of unproductive behavior. The counselor was unsure about the level of unproductive behavior. There seemed to be indications from Mr. H of a willingness to care for Mrs. H, but at the same time his depressed feelings seemed to indicate that he wanted to get rid of the responsibility of taking care of his wife during the demanding time of her recovery.

- After three sessions with Mr. H the counselor suggested that he bring his wife with him to the next session. At this session the two were asked their views of their problem and specifically Mr. H's depression. Mr. H repeated his earlier feelings about Mrs. H's need for watchful care. Mrs. H disagreed strongly and insisted that he get out of the apartment more and visit his friends. This was new information.

- Observe carefully the action-feedback-action process of the marital system. Mrs. H's condition required more responsibility taking for Mr. H. Her illness was responded to with depressed feelings from Mr. H. His depression in turn made it more difficult for her to get well. As her recovery was extended, his depression got worse. The reverberations were felt 500 miles away. The daughters came home to care for the parents. Mr. H's depression did not improve. Even after they went back to their homes, they telephoned each night. Mr. H's level of unproductive behavior was becoming more clear. He seemed at this point and in this context to be at level 4, withdrawing from responsibility.

• Encourage Mrs. H to be warm and understanding to Mr. H but to avoid letting him off the responsibility "hook."

• Bring daughters into session when they come home to visit and encourage them to continue to be warm but not to rescue their father from responsibility.

• Encourage Mr. H by using contract with positive and negative reinforcers.

SITUATION 3: CHRONIC COMPLAINER

Mr. F is an 84-year-old widower. His parents came to the United States from Italy when he was a small boy. He can speak English but has a heavy accent and is sometimes difficult to understand. He owned a local business before he sold it at age 75 when he felt it became too much for him to look after. He had been married for 40 years to a woman who looked after his every need. Mr. F was the second child in a family of six children, all the others being females. Even though he was the second child, he was treated as if he were the first child since he was the only male.

Mr. F is a very popular attender at the local senior citizen's weekly dinner meetings. He even went on a special travel excursion to New York City that the local AARP chapter sponsored. He remains very mobile and apparently is in good health, but he is constantly complaining about everything, including his health, his income, the food at the weekly dinners, the lack of attention from his children, and the like. He seems to linger on his problems and talk of nothing else during a conversation. Neighbors check on him regularly. One of Mr. F's biggest problems is his manipulation of people by making them feel sorry for him. He calls on different agencies in the community for food, money, and fuel. He gets very angry when an agency sends him canned food instead of bread and meat. He has a history of getting other people to handle his affairs. A local agency staff person asked for advice on how to handle the situation. She brought him groceries and household items. He began expecting her delivery and complained when she did not come when he thought she should. After checking his actual financial condition she feels that Mr. F can afford the items himself and that he misses his wife's care so much that he uses sob stories to get others, including herself, to take care of him.

Resolution Process

• Determine the level of unproductive behavior. Some individuals who have contact with Mr. F indicated only mild annoyance at his sob stories. Most of these had only casual informal relationships with Mr. F, like going on the travel excursion with him. The staff person felt Mr. F insisted on controlling her behavior. With casual relationships he was probably at level one, "Attention seeking," but with the staff person he was probably at level two, "Bossy" or controlling.

• Since no formal arrangement exists between the agency and Mr. F, and since he seems to be able to afford items he needs but has developed patterns of controlling people, it was recommended that the staff person decide what she was willing to do with Mr. F. She was not willing to bring him food and household items. She was willing to take Mr. F to the shopping center along with two others who lived near him, twice a week.

• Initiate a friendly offer to Mr. F indicating her willingness to schedule a time to take him with two others to the shopping center twice a week so he could buy the items he needed.

• Explain that she could take him and the other two older persons together at 10:00 A.M. or 3:00 P.M. The three of them could decide which time would be best for all three of them. She would decide the first time just to get them together. Then, while together, they would work out a time suitable to all.

• Encourage social involvement: education classes, volunteer work contributing to others.

The staff person felt better knowing specific procedures she could use that would prevent her from being manipulated. However, she wanted to relate to Mr. F in a way that avoided anger and criticism on her part. The above procedure enabled her to maintain respect for herself and at the same time act toward Mr. F in a way that promoted his independence.

SITUATION 4: WHO HAS THE PHONE?

Mrs. C is 86 and in reasonably good health, has a lot of friends, and is generally cooperative. She is a resident at one of the nursing homes and seems to be adapting to not being in her own home. She fell, broke her hip, and decided herself to enter the home.

One of the privileges the residents of each wing have is to keep a phone in their room for one hour each day to make local calls. Mrs. C had kept the phone in her room, and other residents complained to the supervisor. This had happened for several days. A regular practice of the supervisor coming in to get the phone from Mrs. C began to develop. What should be done?

Resolution Process

• Determine the level of unproductive behavior. The supervisor had got into the practice of reminding Mrs. C about bringing the phone back each day. The reminding pattern seem to be evidence that Mrs. C may be at level one. "Attention getting."

• Work out a contract with Mrs. C with the desired behavior made explicit: Bring the phone back to the office within an hour from the time it was checked out. The positive consequence is use of the phone the next day for one hour. If the phone is kept past one hour the supervisor will come and pick up the phone. The consequence of this is to lose the privilege of using the phone the next day.

• If Mrs. C loses phone privileges for one day, she should be told that she can begin again the day following the loss of the privilege.

• Encourage more social involvement, perhaps some volunteer time helping others.

SITUATION 5: WHO WILL BRUSH MY HAIR?

Mrs. L is a 75-year-old middle-class widow. She had lived with her daughter's family since she fell and broke her hip. Before that she had kept her own house and was active in clubs and community groups. Since the fall she has displayed more dependent behavior. One of the problems that gripes her daughter is her mother's insistence that her daughter brush her hair for her. She knows her mother can brush it, but will not do it when she is around.

Resolution Process

• Determine level of unproductive behavior. The daughter's response to her mother is primarily annoyance. Consequently, the goal of her mother's behavior appears to be attention getting.

• The daughter should tell her mother (at a time other than when the hairbrushing request occurs) that she feels she can brush her own hair and for the daughter to continue to do it for her would be to discourage her.

• When a hairbrushing is requested, the daughter should say once, "I think you can handle it, Mother."

• If Mrs. L fusses and complains, the daughter should leave the area and not discuss the issue further as long as there is opportunity to maintain a struggle.

The intervention process exemplified in "you can do it" may bring negative reactions when first used. If the unproductive behavior has been bringing attention up to this point, it will not be given up easily. Expect things to get worse before they get better.

SITUATION 6: REGULAR TELEPHONE CALLING TO STAFF AT HOME

Mrs. C. has been a regular attender for years at the programs offered by the county agency on aging. She has begun lately to call Mrs. Barlow, a staff person at the agency, at home. The first evening call took Mrs. Barlow a little by surprise, and she reluctantly listened to Mrs. C for an hour. Mixed feelings appeared: She felt annoyed that her valuable time at home was being taken by the call. Then she felt a little selfish, considering Mrs. C as probably lonely and in need of someone to talk with. She thought to herself that being nice to Mrs. C would help her through this difficult time and that she would probably not call her any more after work. No call came the next night. Mrs. Barlow felt she had done the right thing and chastised herself for being annoyed. The next night Mrs. C called again. Then again the following night. By this time Mrs. Barlow became not only quite annoyed with Mrs. C but puzzled about what to do with her calling behavior.

Resolution Process

• Determine the level of unproductive behavior. In this case the feelings of Mrs. Barlow reveal the goal of Mrs. C's level of behavior: The feelings of being annoyed indicate the level and goal of the unproductive behavior are "Attention getting."

• Select an appropriate strategy (Chapter 4).

• Normally, ignoring unproductive attention seeking and rewarding constructive respecting behavior would be suggested. However, it would be difficult to ignore a phone call. To fail to answer the phone might risk messages that would be desired. Once the phone has been answered, ignoring is not functional. What would the reader do? Before reading further recall the suggestions from Chapter 4 and try to give a rationale for your selection.

Mrs. Barlow is encouraged to make use of the intervention techniques involving the communication of "I am willing," "I am not willing" to Mrs. C. This response would go something like: I cannot talk with you now, but I am willing to work out a time with you at the office sometime this week. I can meet with you (looking at her appointment book) for 30 minutes, on Wednesday from 10 to 10:30 A.M. or

2:30 to 3:00 P.M. or on Thursday afternoon from 3:30 to 4:00 P.M. Which time would be best for you?

Suppose Mrs. C just keeps on talking and does not respond to the suggestion. Mrs. Barlow has at least two options: She can say, "Do you want to decide or do you want me to decide?" or she can say, "I have to go now. Let me know tomorrow, or my secretary if I am busy, which time is best for you. Goodbye Mrs. C, I look forward to talking with you in more detail at the time you choose." Click.

Some individuals will find this approach uncomfortable at first. One reason is the unfortunate captivity to the "love mistake." The attention-getting behavior is counterproductive for Mrs. C. Reinforcing this pattern (listening at home) encourages Mrs. C to continue the unproductive behavior. The recommendation is designed to act in behalf of her growth.

SITUATION 7: 45 MINUTES TO VISIT—ENTRAPPED INTO TWO-HOUR SESSION

Mrs. B, 67 years old, came to visit her friend Mrs. D, also 67. Mrs. B had only about 45 minutes. She had promised some other friends that she would take them to town shopping. Mrs. D was so glad to see her and insisted on fixing tea for their visit. By the time the water was hot and the tea was served, 30 minutes had passed. Then Mrs. D began talking about her grandchildren and insisted that Mrs. B look through her bulging picture album. Mrs. B, a very gentle, giving person, was beginning to feel very anxious and out of control of events. She has felt this same thing happening with her and Mrs. D every time she comes to visit. What should she do? She has always knuckled under in the past but hated it.

Resolution Process

• Determine the level of unproductive behavior. Mrs. B feels out of control and we could infer that more than likely she is feeling, also, a need to reassert her control over the situation. This tells us that Mrs. D is at level two with Mrs. B, acting out a kind or bossy, controlling behavior.

• Chapter 4 suggests a number of intervention techniques, contracting and assertiveness. Because of the nonregularity of contacts between Mrs. B and Mrs. D, a contract would not be very useful.

• A combination of assertiveness and encouragement techniques would be helpful. Mrs. B should state clearly and assertively that she has 45 minutes to visit, then she has to leave to meet a commitment (and be sure to leave at the end of 45 minutes or else Mrs. D will never believe her or take her seriously the next time). Mrs. B could say, "Would you like me to use the 45 minutes looking at the album or is there anything else you would like to talk about for part of the time?" Encourage activity that gets her involved in helping others.

SITUATION 8: REFUSAL TO USE CRAYONS AND COLORING BOOK

Mrs. J, thinking she has the best interests of the older residents in mind, has purchased crayons and a number of coloring books for the older persons to color during recreation time. Mr. C refuses to participate, calling the practice childish recreation. Mrs. J, who feels she should not tax the older persons, felt just keeping them busy would take their minds off themselves. She has become very annoyed at Mr. C's refusal to participate.

Resolution Process

• Stop treating the old persons as children. This encourages noncooperation, increased dependence, lowered self-concept, and saps the capacity for independence.

• Encourage decision making on the part of the elderly (this practice shows respect for them as persons and keeps them more active mentally). Bring in several options for recreation and allow the individuals to choose.

• Ask for suggestions if options are not readily seen.

• Encourage involvement by the older persons in deciding themselves: how long the recreation period should be; how many different activities are desired each day; how to take turns having suggestions for different activities carried out so everyone is treated fairly; and so on. The more decisions the older persons make, the more they will participate and support the activity.

SITUATION 9: MRS. K TAKES OVER

At the nutrition program site (lunch and program) Mrs. K has been a persistent problem to the staff. She takes over as soon as she arrives in the morning. Many of the others have complained to the staff, but nothing seems to help. One staff member tried to divert her attention hoping she would then leave her older peers alone. That seemed to work for about 30 minutes. Ignoring Mrs. K did not help either.

Resolution Process

• Determine the level of unproductive behavior. The staff at the nutrition site was continually feeling a need to take back the authority that Mrs. K had assumed. The evidence seemed clear: the level of unproductive behavior was "Bossy," control. What was not so clear was the extent this behavior was displayed. The staff had seen bossy behavior before, but never to this degree.

• Find more information about Mrs. K's family history (Chapter 3). It was discovered that Mrs. K was the oldest sister of three younger siblings. She had become a quasi-parent when she was very young and had been reinforced by her parents for being so responsible. She had grown up accustomed to telling her sisters what to do. In Mrs. K's private logic, taking over at the nutrition site was natural and behavior to be expected of her.

• Discuss beforehand with the staff what things to which Mrs. K's organizational ability might be usefully applied.

• Point out useful aspects of Mrs. K's organizational abilities and ask her if she would be willing to use her potential in several areas (options chosen beforehand). Give her a choice, then expect her to do those.

• If Mrs. K moves out of these bounds, set a time for a staff person to meet with her and construct a contract with positive consequences for keeping to her commitments and negative consequences if she breaks her agreement (see Chapter 4 for contract construction).

It is very important not to discourage Mrs. K's growth, and it is equally important not to allow Mrs. K to discourage her peers' growth. The contract is especially helpful for presuming and establishing the rights of all parties involved.

SITUATION 10: UNCOOPERATIVENESS

Mrs. J, 72 years of age, with a high school education, widowed, and the youngest child of a four-child family, is now living with her daughter's family. Mrs. J eats lunch at the Diner's Club (congregate meal program for the elderly) and will not cooperate with others in helping set the table or clean up after lunch. It appears that Mrs. J enjoys being waited on and having others take care of the routine tasks that need to be done. The meaning of this behavior is understood more clearly by Mrs. J's family position. She was the youngest in her family, was babied as a child, and taken care of by her parents, two older sisters, and a brother. She grew up in the formative years counting on being taken care of. This style of life continues now in her later years. Others around her do not like Mrs. J to expect them to wait on her and to fulfill her responsibility in cleaning up after the meal.

On the one hand Mrs. J's behavior appears queenlike, expecting others to serve her. Having had a family context that did let her off the responsibility hook, she did not develop her own skills in coping with tasks. Alongside the queenlike behavior Mrs. J has a lot of inadequate feelings about being able to cope with responsibility. We know more about the dynamics of Mrs. J's problem, but what can be done to help her become more responsible for her own behavior?

Resolution Process

• Determine the level of unproductive behavior. It could be that Mrs. J is engaged in attention getting, wanting to feel special, and is willing to take the negative reactions in order to maintain her position as a queen figure being taken care of. She might be saying to her peers and the staff, I will show you that I do not have to follow your rules. I can be a bigger boss than you. Or, she may feel that she has been given responsibilities that are the lowest in status. Feeling hurt, she may feel a desire to "Counter-hurt" by not doing the jobs. It could be she is acting out "Disablement," saying, in effect, "Get off my back. Do not expect anything of me." The level became more clear when the group members expressed hurt feelings from Mrs. J's behavior. It became clear this was the goal of Mrs. J: to hurt back because she felt she had been hurt by having been assigned arbitrarily a low-status task. She felt she would be stuck forever with that task if she took it. The level of unproductive behavior suggested a need to restructure the nature of the relationships among the club members, particularly with respect to responsibility expectations.

• Have the members of the club meet to discuss the general problem of responsibility for the club.

• Have the members help draw up a list of *all* the specific jobs that are required for the club to function.

• Ask members if they would be willing to work together to assume the responsibilities necessary for the club to continue.

• Allow the group to choose the responsibilities they would be willing to assume.

• In order to give everyone a fair chance at not being saddled with a disagreeable task, allow the group to decide how to rotate tasks and chore selection procedures. Often individuals are unwilling to assume a task because they did not have a choice originally. This was a large part of the problem with Mrs. J. Beginning democratically built a good base of respect for everyone without singling out Mrs. J as the problem. The Mrs. J's of the world ordinarily would be more willing to clean up or set tables under this democratic approach that allows each member to choose responsibilities.

Actually, Mrs. J became more willing to do the table setting and cleaning under the new structure of choosing tasks and having them rotate regularly. If, after this approach was initiated, Mrs. J had refused to assume any responsibility, a contract could have been initiated with positive and negative consequences spelled out and agreed to beforehand (see Chapter 4).

SITUATION 11: REFUSES TO WEAR HEARING AID AT MONTHLY CITIZEN LUNCHEON

Mrs. T, age 68, with an elementary school education, is married and lives with her husband. Her health is good. She is very active, but has a hearing problem. Mrs. T makes little contact with her three children, seven grandchildren, and her brother. The family rarely visits her.

Mrs. T refuses to wear her hearing aid at the monthly senior citizen luncheon and always asks to have all announcements repeated to her privately. She always sits beside the staff director of the local aging agency, who has gotten in the habit of repeating all announcements to Mrs. T.

Resolution Process

• Determine the level of unproductive behavior. The staff director's feelings of annoyance is evidence that the goal of Mrs. T's behavior is most likely "Attention getting."

• Ask Mrs. T (at another time than when the luncheon is in progress) if there is any problem with her hearing aid. If there is none, tell her of the inability to continue repeating all announcements to her.

• Tell Mrs. T that it appears she can handle the announcements on her own with the use of her hearing aid.

• Do not engage in any arguments, defenses, or justifications for the inability to continue to repeat the announcements.

• At the luncheon, resist giving any evidence of avoiding her by sitting somewhere else.

• At the luncheon, if requests are made for repeating announcements, ignore them.

• Give attention to Mrs. T when she is not engaging in unproductive attention seeking.

By ignoring Mrs. T's questions for repeats at the luncheon, she will be encouraged to make a conscious choice of using the hearing aid and thereby take more responsibility for her own life. Her leaning on others helps to lower her self-concept and capacity for independence. By refusing to give attention to unproductive behavior and making sure to give attention when she is not demanding it, the staff person is expressing growth-building care for Mrs. T.

SITUATION 12: THE CHILD BECOMES THE PARENT

Mr. B, 76, and Mrs. Q, 71, both widowed, have discovered, with delight, each other's company. They met at the senior citizen center and now spend most of their time doing things together. Their spirits have risen. Excitement permeates their lives once again. They are like young lovers. Other seniors in the center like both of them and approve heartily of the developing relationship.

Mr. B's daughter, now 46, has called on the senior citizen center director, virtually demanding that she do all in her power to terminate her father's love affair. The daughter insists that Mrs. Q is only after his money.

Resolution Process

Since Mr. B and Mrs. Q are engaging in normal age-specific behavior without interfering with the needs of others, including Mr. B's daughter, there is no problem with unproductive behavior. It is recommended that the senior citizen center director not get involved.

SITUATION 13: LEAVE ME ALONE, BUT NOT COMPLETELY

Mr. T. is 67 years old, grew up as an only child, finished one year of college, is now widowed, and has one child and one grandchild. None of his family lives within 400 miles. His current health status is fair to good. He gets little exercise and has recurring flu and colds. He has been at the nursing home for one year and has gradually withdrawn from all activities. He eats all meals in his room and, when neither eating nor sleeping, sits in a chair and stares. No one asks or expects anything of Mr. T anymore. Staff members continue to try to get through to Mr. T, but he does not respond. The only response anyone has gotten from him occurred one day when he was offered chocolate candy from a birthday box for a staff member.

The specific problem with respect to Mr. T is the virtual helplessness pattern he has developed. One staff person could keep busy just taking care of his needs. Many have tried to talk him out of his withdrawal. Others have lectured him, but the response of most is, "I give up. I cannot do anything with him."

Resolution Process

• Determine the level of unproductive behavior. The response "I give up" is evidence that the goal of Mr. T is actually to have others give up on him, but not completely. He has everyone doing for him and apparently does not wish this to stop. His actions indicate that he only wishes not to have anything expected of him. The level of unproductive behavior is four, "Disablement." The remedial suggestions appropriate at the first three levels may not get constructive response given this condition. Mr. T would probably not respond now to democratic, respect-oriented initiatives.

• Select one staff person to work with Mr. T more closely.

• Construct a series of steps specifically defining desirable behavior for Mr. T. Order the steps beginning with simple responses and successively increasing the expectations. The list might be:

1. Looking at individuals who pass by his door.
2. Sitting in a chair just outside his room and looking at people who pass by.
3. Sitting on the outer edge of the large recreation room, looking at the individuals in the room.
4. Sitting with a group of individuals in the recreation room.
5. Imitating any action of a member of the group.
6. Make a one-word verbal response to any question of a staff member.
7. Giving a verbal response of three or more words to a staff member's question.
8. Initiating a conversation with a staff member.
9. Respond to a question by another resident.
10. Initiate a conversation with another resident.
11. Take one meal in the common dining hall.
12. Participate cooperatively in a group activity.
13. Take two meals in the dining hall.
14. Take three meals in the dining hall.

This approach is called *shaping*, and greater detail can be found in any book on behavior modification.

• Select reinforcers to be used with Mr. T. One obvious resource for Mr. T is the chocolate candy. Careful study of Mr. T's behavior and the services performed for him will reveal other potential reinforcing agents.

• A strict reinforcement process must be followed: (1) The successive approximations of desired behavior must be reinforced immediately as they occur. (2) The desired behavior must be appropriately reinforced. If a behavior is reinforced for too long a period, it may become fixed at that stage and successive steps may not occur. Further, if the shaping process of the steps is too slow, the individual may not respond; or if shaping occurs too rapidly, the earlier shaped behavior may disappear.

• Begin reinforcement. The staff person might begin the process by saying, "I certainly like it when I come by your room on my way to the office and you are sitting looking toward the door so I can see you."

• Begin democratic, respect-oriented strategies after Mr. T has been through all the steps of the reinforcement program.

• Organize community support system for encouragement toward increasing educational and social skills.

SITUATION 14: INADEQUATE DIET

Mrs. L, 73, lives alone after the death of her husband. Her closest family member lives 350 miles from her, coming to visit about every six months. She complained of blackout spells to her doctor. The diagnosis was simple: inadequate diet. The doctor recommended a diet for Mrs. L that would include all her daily requirements. To support his efforts he called the nutrition site center and asked for help in signing up Mrs. L for the hot meal program. The staff person called on Mrs. L, told her the bus schedule for the noon meal and invited her to participate. Mrs. L began to participate in the hot meal program. This gave the staff person an opportunity to talk with her about her diet. She found that, despite her doctor's advice, Mrs. L was not eating any more than the one hot meal a day and getting by on snacks or nothing at all the rest of the day. When asked about the inadequate diet, she said that she couldn't push herself to cook just for herself now that her husband had died. She knew she should eat better but somehow lacked the motivation. The staff person found herself continually reminding Mrs. L to watch her diet.

Resolution Process

• Determine the level of unproductive behavior. Mrs. L seems to be engaging in attention-getting behavior. This conclusion is reinforced by the staff person's feeling of a need to remind.

• Construct an individual contract with Mrs. L. The desirable behavior would be defined as fulfilling the doctor's recommended diet. Positive consequences for daily observance of the diet requirements are to be drawn up along with negative consequences if it it not fulfilled daily (see Chapter 4 for details of construction).

• Organize community support system for encouraging development of social and educational skills.

SITUATION 15: KEEP REMINDING ME

Mr. W, 74, and his wife have been regular attenders at the senior citizen center weekly meetings. Recently the center changed directors. Mr. W missed a meeting and called the new director, whom he had met when she first came three weeks ago. He gently chided her for not calling him about the weekly meeting. The next week the director called Mr. W the day before the meeting to remind him. After the meeting was over Mr. W told the director to be sure and call him the day before the next meeting. Several others, overhearing Mr. W, also asked her to call them. The director had announced the meeting for the next week just prior to adjournment. Why, she thought, in a faintly annoyed frame of mind, would he need to be reminded again? She called the previous director about the practice of reminding. The previous director said she had not had to remind Mr. and Mrs. W, or others, and that they had been very regular in attendance. The new director decided she had better check with her board of directors about the practice. She did not want to get into the reminding habit but she wanted the support of her board. Several members were contacted. One thought the center would lose a lot of attenders if she did not call and remind the older people. "After all," she said, "old people don't remember things as well as they used to." The second board member encouraged her to do what she thought best. What should she do?

Resolution Process

• Determine the level of unproductive behavior. The reminding is good evidence that Mr. W's problem is at level one, attention getting.

• At a meeting, during the period when the director usually announced the next week's meeting, the director should tell the group what she is willing to do about reminding.

• Tell the group she is quite willing to continue announcing the next week's meeting during the program, but that she was having problems about an additional reminder during the week. "I do not like what it means when I call and remind people about the meeting. It says to me that I do not respect your ability to remember for one week, that I think of you as children. This undermining of your self-confidence bothers me. Therefore, I have decided that I would feel better, and that it would be more of an act of genuine caring for you if I stop treating you like children by reminding you of our meeting. I really feel that you can manage this remembering task quite well."

• Do no more calling after the announcement is made at the meeting. Aside from declines associated with aging, one of the major reasons individuals do not remember is that they have not been pushed to have to exercise this ability. The human brain has potential for retention. The capacity has fallen into disuse because of increasing reliance on technological substitutes: endless reminders from TV, magazines, newspapers, radio, billboards, etc. The "Griot," a vital link in Alex Haley's *Roots*, had committed to memory details of village history that spanned 200 years! Many of the historical links to prehistory (period prior to systematic record keeping) were made possible by oral history —that is, the commitment to memory of incredible amounts of detail over long periods of time.

The gentle but firm nudgings that encourage increased development of older persons' potential is a contribution toward their prolonged independence. This requires as much a change of attitude on our part as it does the development of the skill to do it.

SITUATION 16: TRAPPED BY THE TALKER

Mr. A, 80 years of age, regularly stands around the nursing home office looking for someone to talk to. He ties up staff in conversations and they are not able to get their work done. They do not know how to respond to him without hurting his feelings. A number of people have complained about him. Nothing other than a long-term conversation will satisfy him. The more time spent, the more time he seems to demand. His behavior is very irritating to a number of employees who work at the home.

Resolution Process

• Determine the level of unproductive behavior. The response of the employees to Mr. A is most closely identified with attention getting.

• Do not reinforce irritating "talking" behavior. When he is standing around the office looking for someone to talk to, do not respond. When he is in other places or is involved in other activities, give him a great deal of attention.

• Involve Mr. A in a group reminiscence activity. The following may serve as examples:

1. Group meetings to discuss an old film that has just been shown.
2. Group reminiscence about past events such as wars, the depression, certain years (40s, 50s, and clothing styles, transportation, and so on).
3. Listening and discussing old records. The records would be played. Then reflection upon the past could focus on dates, meanings, and events that occurred during that period of time.

Having Mr. A in a group is designed to help satisfy his needs to belong and be involved. This is a positive process to accompany the lack of reinforcement of the unproductive behavior. It is important that all the employees be informed about the approach and cooperate.

SITUATION 17: LIFE IS ALWAYS SEEN AS BLEAK

Mrs. V, age 62, has cancer of the lung. She is in pain some of the time. The rest of her time is spent telling others about the horrible fate that awaits her. Each day brings nothing new or good for her. Her four children hate to visit her because of her bleak future, which she constantly reminds them of. The feeling is one of being irritated and annoyed, with a tendency to remind her about what good things she does have.

Resolution Process

• Determine the level of unproductive behavior. The evidence points strongly to attention getting.

• Lead Mrs. V in a guided reflection on pleasant past experiences as a type of life review. As a mother of four children, there must be many memories and experiences from past years that have brought great joys into her life. It may be most beneficial for the children to collect pictures, relics, and other material from years past, for use in stimulating thinking of pleasant experiences.

Some items could include:

1. Pictures, with appropriate questions such as (a) Mother, remember when you were married? What was it like to be in love then? (b) Look at this car! Can you remember your first automobile ride? Where did you go? What kind of car was it? What color? (c) Mother, look at these pictures of old houses! How were homes built then? Do you really think they were different from what they are now?

2. Old magazines or newspaper articles. (a) Look at these headlines! Can you remember what you were doing the day World War II started? Ended? (b) Where were you when you saw your first airplane? How old were you at the time? What color was the plane? Have you ever ridden in an airplane?
3. Reflection upon past experiences. (a) Mother, can you remember when we went to Carlsbad Caverns? (b) How about the time we went to visit Uncle Bill and his family? (c) Remember when Aunt Sue burned the Thanksgiving turkey? Everyone was so discouraged because they thought the family reunion was spoiled, and you saved it by bringing out the country hams you had stored.

In order to use reminiscence effectively, there must be attention given to the development of activities meaningful to the involved individual. What some would find very pleasant to reflect upon, others would not enjoy in the least. It is, therefore, necessary to know as much as possible about the past experiences of the individuals with whom you are working. Once an awareness of past historical events has been established, appropriate questions may be developed.

For people such as Mrs. V, a retreat from the present to the past may be a most refreshing venture. It may quiet her in pulling together experiences and thus reinforce her capacity to cope with life. Family cohesiveness may also develop through reflections upon the past. Just as most people enjoy reminiscing with a group of high school or perhaps service friends, so it is pleasant to think back on family experiences.

There is no getting around the fact that Mrs. V has cancer of the lung and her days probably *are* numbered. She also has pain, and most people would have little difficulty understanding why she acts the way she does. At the same time, it is the responsibility of those around her to help her live, as best she can, the rest of her life with as much coping ability as possible.

- Organize community support system for social interaction, physical and medical needs, and possibility of contributions she can make (sewing, knitting, phoning, etc.).

SUMMARY

The case studies given reflect a general variety of problems that are typical among the elderly population. These problems are described as typical, not normal. The reason they are not seen as normal is that they are primarily the result of an attitude toward older persons in our culture and a pattern of feedback that contributes to the problem. They do not necessarily reflect any universal problem innate to individuals who are aging. When elderly persons display childlike problems of unproductive behavior, they are reflecting the cultural context in which individuals age. The behaviors then are typical of a social milieu that discourages responsibility taking and encourages dependence. One inference we may draw is this: Older persons in a different social environment would not necessarily act out the problems presented. But since changing an entire culture is a bit overwhelming, we can intervene within specific family and social systems to help bring about courage and responsible freedom on a smaller scale among individuals in that portion of the culture that we occupy. An approach to greater freedom and independence on a group level will be discussed in Chapter 6.

Chapter 6
Group Structures Promote Independence

Only 5 percent of all elderly reside in group institutional settings, but this actual number is sizable. Nursing home facilities have mushroomed in the past decade, and greater numbers can now receive these benefits through government Medicare and Medicaid programs. While new buildings multiply and large numbers of staff persons are recruited to supply the nursing home facilities, staff training often suffers. The need for profits means that many nursing home owners are reluctant to budget funds for training programs. Individuals are hired and—with their random backgrounds, biases, taboos, and myths—are often turned loose as the primary agents of care for the complex problems of an elderly population. Few, if any, standards exist in terms of education and human relations training. This can result in unwitting reinforcement of dependency, loss of self-confidence, and lack of independence motivation. Without training, staff often resort to the demeaning approaches associated with dependency training of children: The staff makes the rules and the elderly adjust or else! It should not surprise us that so many problems of uncooperativeness, withdrawal, revenge, and annoyance behaviors occur. These are some of the forms that rebellion against disrespect takes at this stage of the life cycle.

Individuals who spend a portion of their later years in institutional settings will retain a sense of personhood to the extent they are *participants* in a social system. This involvement necessitates the attainment and maintenance of selected tangible and intangible symbols of participation (Henry, 1965). To the extent that these symbols are not present, the process of depersonalization is enhanced. Rodstein et al. (1976) found that the less capable the new patient was of maintaining autonomous activity, the more likely would it be the patient would experience severe adjustment problems during the first year. In that same research study Rodstein (1976) found that by challenging the older person to increase control over his or her own life, improvement in adjustment would occur. Said another way, the greater the amount of involvement, the greater the feelings of belonging and independence (Romney, 1970). Filer and O'Connell (1964) found that residents were positively motivated through daily performance of constructive work. Bayne (1970) suggested that the dependency, apathy, and withdrawal of elderly residents in nursing homes may be a function of their accommodation to an environment that encourages the sick role by denying them enough responsibility for the regulation and control of their environment.

Felton and Kahana (1974) showed that the incongruence created by an incoming patient's internal locus of control and institutional expectations of control over the patient results in a loss of self-direction, which is linked to adjustment problems. Giordano and Giordano (1972) demonstrated improved morale in patients as they were drawn into active participation in decision making among residents. Kantor, Hiller, and Thuell (1974) found improved staff-patient relations when patients were involved in self-directing programs. This occurred in spite of staff prejudices against the program's initiation. Abdo et al. (1973) demonstrated significantly better adjustment among widows involved in a self-governing public housing environment as compared with widows in an institutional setting without self-governing opportunities. Heumann (1978) proposed a conceptual innovation for elderly who are not familiar with the new responsibilities a residential home for the elderly might offer. He suggested a more individualized responsibility assignment that, taken in steps, would be described as "assisted independent living." The physical, cognitive, and emotional state of each individual would guide the level and type of involvement.

Nursing home owners often create their own problems by refusing to insist on staff training. In the long haul they pay more than the price training would have cost and, moreover, have low morale, anger, and disruptiveness.

With properly trained staff a nursing home could tap invaluable independence resources among its residents and thus conceivably could lower costs by reducing the number of staff. Training in methods designed to "win" cooperation offers new vistas in nursing home atmosphere and governance. Many of these strategies have been discussed in previous chapters. A special group intervention approach is needed to enhance self-respect, assumption of responsibility, and the development of continued independence and cooperation.

NURSING HOME ASSEMBLY*

One medium for training in democratic living, mutual respect, and cooperation is a nursing home assembly. In most nursing homes the number of residents is too large to have one assembly that includes everyone. A structure in which a small number of elected or appointed individuals attempt to represent the larger group is inadequate if it is the only democratic process. What seems to work best is a breakdown of the total number of residents into semi-independent assemblies according to logical residence patterns within the home. For example, a *wing assembly*, reflecting one wing of a nursing home spread, might be one format. In a high-rise structure, a *floor council* might seem more appropriate.

The assembly allows each individual to have input with respect to his or her particular concerns. A nursing home population without prior experience in living with each other will not be as responsive to a representative-type organization. They tend to discount this structure as capable of adequately reflecting their individual concerns.

Assuming that a basic level of assembly is in operation, these groups may want to have representation on a council that could coordinate the concerns of each assembly for establishment of overall home policy.

The intent of this approach is not to take over control of nursing homes. Nor is it assumed that a pure democracy is advisable. There may be, and usually are, rules and regulations that the nursing home staff has no control over. It is obvious that the assembly would recognize this limitation on its deliberations. But there are many rules and policies in nursing homes that could well be decided by the residents. These areas could be addressed by the assemblies. One wing or floor assembly could conceivably develop some policies for its residents that would be different from another assembly. There seems to be no enormous problem with allowing such potential differences. The im-

* This concept is based on the principles of the family council (Dreikurs, Gould, & Corsini, 1974).

portant aspect would be the infusion of some control over their existence that is so rare in institutional settings.

The assembly is based on several assumptions. First, all nursing home residents are to be treated equally. All nursing home residents should be respected and show respect. Nursing home policy is the business of all residents. Finally, problems in a nursing home can be best worked out when all residents work on them.

Although the nursing home has been developed by individual owners, this does not give them the right of absolute control over its occupants. Residents make their contributions to the continuing development of the home, and therefore it can be said that, to a degree, it belongs to all members. Many nursing home owners and staff members see themselves as having total responsibility for the residents. Residents are consequently often shielded from the real world, and their dependence is encouraged. The staff does not like what it has created, usually. When residents begin to expect to have everything done for them, the staff members complain that they are not more independent. To counter the expectations (which the actions of staff can help create), staff members often adopt disrespecting strategies to keep the old people in control, to keep them down. At the same time the residents see those on the staff as their enemies, to be defeated and undermined. Each reinforces the other's interaction and feedback.

As nursing home staff members begin to see the older persons as their equals (having equal claims to respect and dignity), they can also expect from them cooperative responses to the functioning of the nursing home. As this occurs, they will discover the advantages of a democratic approach to residential living.

The purpose of an assembly is to intervene in the system processes of unproductive behavior feedback loops. This process helps provide a feeling of togetherness and a means of respecting the human dignity of each resident. Any resident should have a say in decisions that affect him or her. The assembly is not to be seen as a new technique for nursing home staff members to force compliance to their already-decided policies. It is to be an experience in sharing and a practice in learning to make effective decisions. Specifically, the assembly's purpose is to make decisions and solve problems that affect residents. Who, for example, could know better than residents when and how long visiting hours should be? Further, the assembly allows residents opportunities to share good news about themselves—for example, grandchildren, special occasions, accomplishments, and so on. The assembly can provide an outlet for discussing a personal decision or obtaining constructive problem-solving feedback.

There are several basic guiding principles. The goal of the assembly is to work things out. No one should feel put down or taken advantage of. If this does occur, uncooperativess is likely to be the outcome. Once a problem is presented, a helpful phrase that sets a healthy atmosphere is, "What can *we* do about it?" The residents share a common experience. What affects one to some degree affects all of them. Individual problems are actually group problems. Throughout the meeting mutual respect and caring should be evident. It is desirable to convey a feeling that "We are all together in this home (wing, floor)." All ideas are important and deserve to be listened to. Accusations and judgments are to be avoided.

Policy decisions and rules should be made by consensus vote. This is to keep from reinforcing an uncooperative minority, with some residents ganging up against the staff or vice versa. The equal vote of everyone encourages more serious consideration of the problem.

If a decision by consensus is not forthcoming, then the chairman announces, "We have not been able to arrive at consensus about our current problem, so we will have to continue the present policy until our next meeting." Blaming is discouraged, and each member is encouraged to say only what he is willing to do and how he feels and not what other members should do.

The assembly meeting is usually run by parliamentary procedure. Rules of order keep the meeting running smoothly. The idea of the assembly can be broached to individuals on the wing or floor. A date is set for the first meeting, and attention is given to a time that is best for everyone. The residents and staff should be invited to attend the first meeting. It is important to convey that attendance is not required but that decisions will be made with regard to policy regardless of how many residents attend.

A temporary presiding chairperson should be selected, someone to keep order and allow everyone an opportunity to speak. The presiding officer is sometimes called a chairperson, moderator, or leader. A secretary is helpful for keeping a record of the discussion and policy agreed upon. Other leadership roles are selected as needed. All the officers are to rotate. The period of time for each office varies from a week to a month. It is best to establish at the beginning that each office is to be rotated.

A staff person may have to organize the first meeting, but he or she should quickly allow the residents to assume responsibility. The staff need not fear that the residents will take complete control. The ground rules require a unanimous vote, not a majority. Suppose the residents decide that all residents should have color TV sets in their rooms instead of only having sets in a TV viewing room. Does that mean the staff have to resort to absolute control again and abolish the democratic assembly? Of course not. Since the vote requires consensus, the staff's rights are protected. The consensus vote also protects the rights of the residents. The consensus vote encourages cooperation between staff and residents.

Other ground rules include a regular time and place to meet. It is important to keep the same meeting time and avoid postponements and emergency meetings.

The first meeting would probably involve an explanation of the new approach. The staff person organizing the meeting could delineate the areas of the nursing home policy that the staff has no control over. The areas that can be decided by the assembly could be talked about.

The assembly can discuss suggestions and plan for entertainment and fun experiences.

The minutes of the meeting can be posted on a bulletin board convenient for all residents to refer to. Some assembly groups have found a suggestion box helpful for placing topics for discussion at the next weekly meeting.

There is no set order for conducting the assembly meetings. Generally, the minutes of the last meeting are read. Dealing with "old business" and "new business" is one way of structuring the meeting. Others have found a helpful structure in discussing the last week's activities and planning for the next week. The meetings should last no longer than 45 minutes to an hour.

Nursing homes will find business grinding a little slower with this approach. But there will be such renewed interest and stimulation to respect and independence that the lost time will be a small price to pay. Staff members carry a heavy burden when they feel they must bear complete responsibility for the home, residents, and policymaking. By allowing the residents to participate through the assembly the responsibility load is shared. Residents, when so respected, will begin to feel a responsibility to help encourage cooperation and support. If the residents participate in policymaking, they will feel more responsiblility for supporting it.

If the nursing home is interested in stimulating and prolonging freedom and independence, this approach will be a must. It has untold potential for encouraging older persons and creating an exciting atmosphere of community living in a nursing home environment.

ADJUSTING TO LONG-TERM CARE

Moving out of one's own home—away from memories, independence, and experiences—can be unsettling. If there have been problems of coping with one's own independent residential living or health problems, moving to a long-term care facility can have its attractions. Nevertheless, moving into a strange community where relationships among the other residents are well established is not an easy accommodation.

The programs of long-term facilities for orientation for new residents are varied, but they have one fairly common element: They are coordinated primarily by staff. The assembly offers a creative new approach to adjustment to long-term care. New residents will need to get acquainted with the staff, but the most important circles to break into, and usually the most difficult, are among the residents themselves.

The staff could coordinate its orientation to long-term care with the assembly to which the new resident will belong. With information supplied by the staff the assembly can get an idea of the interests, activities, and skills of the new resident. They could discuss their own feelings as a new resident and plan for a smooth transition as the resident arrives. Contact could even be made prior to the move with some type of welcoming message that would indicate that the assembly anticipates the resident's coming. It might help to communicate an appreciation of the new person's potential for making their facility more responsive to resident's needs for freedom, respect, and independence as well as physical care.

With an assembly-type structure, the concerns of the residents can be mobilized to bring to bear a significant resource for belonging in the more difficult early weeks of transition. The further usefulness of this model can be seen in the following case study.

CASE STUDY OF RESIDENT GOVERNANCE

There are some institutional settings that have had the courage to explore the potential of resident governance. One example of such a venturesome staff is the Patrick Henry Hospital in Newport News, Virginia. A variation of the assembly model has been put into practice.

The hospital has 356 beds, with slightly more than 75 percent of its patients over 65 years of age. The remainder are younger, chronically ill patients ranging from cases of muscular dystrophy to retardation.

The staff had spent five months classifying patients by care required. The resources of the hospital pushed this type of clarification. One long hall (510 feet) had two nursing stations. There had been random placements of patients on this one floor including patients with minimal care needs and those with skilled care needs. The nurses needed skateboards to cover the area adequately.

The placement of patients by level of care required resulted in four categories: (1) minimal care, (2) support and rehabilitation, (3) complete and total care, and (4) skilled care. All minimal-care patients were placed on the one long floor with only two nursing stations. The staff was decreased in that section and increased in sections 3 and 4, where they were more needed. Nurses are rotated in all four groups to break potential cliques and to distribute the skills over all groups. A task force representing all areas currently reviews all admissions.

The staff's desire to involve residents in participatory governance began with a patient advisory council model. The members were nominated by a few more vocal residents and from the beginning did not have the full support of all of the residents. The council would call secret meetings. The staff members were not tuned in completely to the council, and soon the idea flopped. The concern was still present but the form for involving everyone was yet to be found.

The staff began referring to the residents and themselves as a community. Soon the implications of community began to result in concrete ideas. The residents suggested that the many wings and sections of the hospital be referred to as streets, avenues, and boulevards. The residents on each wing got together and decided on a street name for their wing. This brought a sense of the real world into an institutional setting. Mail was delivered in care of the hospital to the new "street" address. Names of streets were posted in hallways. The practice resulted in more efficient directions for visitors as well as bringing more reality metaphors into the life of the residents.

The next step that evolved from the emerging community was a need for a form of governance in which every resident could experience a form of representation. The idea emerged: Since a town concept had emerged from the street naming, perhaps a town council would work. The mayor of Newport News was asked to come to the hospital and explain the structure of city government. This was the kicker. The new streets were divided into precincts and council members were to be elected from the precincts. All the precincts would elect a mayor and vice-mayor. There were two streets in each precinct and a total of five precincts. Each precinct matched one street of more ambulatory patients with a street with less ambulatory residents. This was done to broaden the concerns of elected council members.

At the beginning of the experiment very few residents could be encouraged to run for office. Those who were willing to run had taken notes from the local politicians. They mounted campaigns for votes with posters and visits to residents in their precincts. The U.S. congressman from the Newport News district came to install the new officers of the Patrick Henry Hospital "Town Council." By the time of the next election there were numbers of candidates desiring to run for office. They knew by now it was going to work, and they wanted to be a part of it. The hospital administrator and nursing director were asked to attend meetings of the council.

Four members of the town council were below 65 years of age, but all were chronically ill. One of the six council members over 65 was a blind double amputee who was 80 years old. At 80 she had started a literary and music group for seven other blind residents.

The functions and concerns of the "town council" extend to all aspects of the hospital. Activities are planned that have included special occasions, such as a Halloween dance with relatives invited to come in costume, a sweetheart dance, and a Las Vegas night, with poker chips and other features. The chips can be turned in for shaving cream, toiletries, cakes, and so on. The "town council" voted to have a limit of two cups of beer, but only for those who would have no problem with beer interfering with medications.

The "town council" also serves to help take the load off staff for governance problems in the hospital. One resident, for example, making use of his creative business skills, set himself up as a parking lot porter and charged fees to visitors on the weekends. This was not a policy of the hospital. This was brought up at the "town council" meeting. It was decided that a democratic approach to solving the problem would be to deal with the issue in terms of a vendor's license. Research had to be done at the Newport News city offices to determine rules involving vendor's licenses. The problem was dealt with without destroying the mental and physical creativity of the residents.

The hospital staff were concerned about a problem of the combination heating and air-conditioning units in the resident rooms. The units were vented at the top, and thus it was possible for liquids to be spilled into the vents, thereby creating a fire hazard. For example, the watering of plants placed on top of the vents created an obvious risk. The staff thought about a direct order to residents to keep things off the units. Instead they took the problem to the council. Some of the council members were very aggressive, insisting that items left on the units be seized. After discussing the issue, the council decided on a memo and precinct visits to all residents to explain the problem. Cooperation was sought rather than compliance demanded. Two weeks for cleaning up the units was suggested. Council members were to visit the precincts to check after the two-week period. Complete cooperation was gained in solving the problem and the independence of the residents was strengthened.

The council offered other advantages. Prior to the council, when a resident died, the room was closed and cleaned out, and then a new resident moved in. This practice gives no opportunity for the resident community to come to grips with the loss of one of their members. It further depersonalizes life. The residents could not help but consider this same thing happening to them when they died. The "town council" addressed itself to this concern. A memorial service in the hospital was suggested. The nurses tuned in to spending more time with the ones who were left. The memorial service allowed the residents and staff to come to grips with their loss. This communicated to the residents a message that they are important. They are cared for.

Working through resident governance is not always easy, especially for those on the nursing staff, who work so closely with residents. One angry double amputee ran away from the home. He was gone for two days. The staff became frantic. Their gut reaction was this: "We have done so much for him. We moved him to an area of the hospital so he could be with his friends, and this is how he pays us back!" The staff decided, arbitrarily, to move his belongings back to his old room. He protested. Then two council members arrived at the scene. They felt his rights were being violated and, very articulately, expressed their fears that the autocratic action of the staff was going to ruin the whole democratic experiment. The staff backed away from their arbitrary decision, reluctantly, and allowed the matter to be taken up by the "town council." The council was not easy on the resident by any means. A contract was formulated to which all parties agreed and signed. The contract contained positive consequences for desirable behavior exhibited and spelled out the negative consequences if the contract was violated. The contract was notarized and the fragile democracy was saved.

The importance of support for democratic governance at the top management level is very important. Inevitably such a group will get into administrative policy. The Patrick Henry administration has not been threatened by this possibility and so far has not had to exercise its veto.

The advantages to overall morale, independence, and increased mental and physical activity make the staff more willing to cooperate as fully as possible. The staff load is much less with the increased feeling of responsibility for each other by the residents. One resident refused to take a bath. The council asked the mayor to visit the resident and encourage him to take his baths for the sake of other residents who had to relate to him. The staff would, consequently, want to encourage the governance of the council.

Before the council developed, the residents were frequently laying out problems to the nurses, asking them what they were going to do about them. Now, with the council, the nurses put this question back to the resident: What have you done about the problem? As a result the residents are doing more for themselves.

The cooperation of the nursing staff is as critical in this approach as that of the top administration. At the beginning of this experiment some nurses were hostile to the idea. It was a different way of thinking. Relating to residents was turned inside out. Much time and effort went into training to obtain the unified approach that is so essential. Some nurses, realizing the program was for real, had to decide to get with it or find another employment setting.

New staff members hired are attracted by an opportunity to be a part of an exciting new program. A staff person is designated to orient new staff in a new version of an old idea: the buddy system. The approach of resident governance is thoroughly explained. High morale among the general staff is encouraged by a type of democratic structure for staff that is evolving as a result of the "town council."

The "town council" has had its problems from time to time. Council members have "taken over" and tried to tell the nurses what to do. On other occasions the council understood the solution to a problem in one way and the nursing staff interpreted the solution in another. These kinds of problems have been returned to the council for solution; for example, a mediation group of council members and nurses was formed to explore problems and seek better communication channels between the nursing staff and the council.

This model seems to have worked exceptionally well for the most part. The level of self-governance in a representative context has been very effective. What has not developed yet is participatory governance on a smaller level (assembly) that would directly involve every individual who is capable of responding. The precinct level could function in this capacity, dealing with its issues of concern by total involvement of residents. The council member could carry its larger concerns to the "town council." Even residents confined to beds could have issues brought to them and their vote taken. Even if they cannot, at the time, coherently deal with the issue, they have received an invaluable message of respect: They matter!

The participatory governance concept is not new to our culture. Its application to all areas of residential and institutional living is yet to be accomplished. The potential for freedom and independence is significant. It is an exciting venture with old people, particularly those who live in institutional settings. A variation of this model can be used with older married couples who remain together in their independent residence.

THE COUPLE CONFERENCE*

Older individuals who live in their homes, as couples, often find that a structure of support helps to ensure that their feedback processes remain constructive and that each has equal access to the marriage rule-making and goal-setting processes. Rather than face endless conflict with neither having his or her needs met, couples frequently make use of a democratic bargaining structure for the improvement of the marriage. This model assumes essentially that neither spouse can have everything desired. They can, however, negotiate in such a manner

* This concept is based on the "couple conference" in Lederer and Jackson (1968).

that each gets the maximum, gets those things which are most important to him or her, while allowing the same for the other.

Usually a meeting time is agreed upon by both partners, with privacy assured. The time of the meeting should be as convenient as possible for both. Many couples have found more progress occurred when an evening was made of it, having dinner out if possible. A relaxed and unhurried atmosphere is essential.

For the first meetings some simple ground rules are helpful. If the meeting is to last for an hour, each spouse is to take 30 minutes. Each can talk or remain silent but cannot be interrupted unless he or she asks. Then the other spouse has a 30-minute period. The major purpose of this ground rule is to emphasize and teach listening. A further ground rule is that each partner will add the words "I feel" before making statements about the other and/or the relationship. The assumption is that everyone has a right to one's own feelings. An individual's feelings are his or her own and have no bearing on the other's.

The next development is for each partner to make the other partner aware of his or her communication patterns, verbal and nonverbal. A coin can be flipped to determine who goes first. One of the most difficult tasks is to isolate the nonverbal ways of communicating—for example, frowns, silence, glazed looks, pretending to listen, muttering incoherently, and so on.

Next the couple needs to make an exhaustive list of all the tasks that must be performed daily and on weekends to keep the home functioning. After the list is completed, they are to take turns selecting the tasks they are willing to carry out. When the tasks have been equally divided, there may remain a few that neither of them wishes to do. This can be solved by each taking a turn for a week. This prevents one spouse from getting stuck with an undesirable but essential task and then feeling put upon.

Regular weekly sessions are to be continued for evaluating the past week's activities and relationship quality and to plan for the coming week. The couple conferences can be used to discuss individual concerns that are not directly related to the other spouse. Entertainment and fun experiences can be planned at these meetings. While couples are starting this structured process for reinforcing each other's rights there is a need for additional involvement that helps focus their thoughts and energies outside themselves.

HELPING OTHERS AS INTERVENTION

Sometimes couples and individuals can become so absorbed with their own needs and rights that life is not very happy or fulfilling. Most therapists agree that life focused on self is a life destined for unhappiness. The healthy life is one focused more on others. It is quite appropriate to give older individuals who are focused on their own troubles an assignment of finding someone who needs them. It does not matter that they may not *feel* like helping others. By the simple act of *doing it*, they will begin to focus less on themselves and their own troubles.

Some old individuals dwell continuously on their complaints and worries. It is as though they enjoy wallowing in their problems and discouragement. Listening to them can be a reinforcing factor, giving attention to a negative approach to life. Motivating the elderly to go find someone they can help, precisely when they are steeped in their own problems, may be the most effective technique we can use at that moment for intervening in their system.

Nursing homes and senior citizen centers would do well to structure programs that involve the elderly helping someone else. The temptation for most programming is to bring in all kinds of individuals to help the elderly. There is nothing wrong with that approach, if it is balanced with a strong emphasis on the elderly being involved in helping others.

Individuals and couples living together can keep themselves in good emotional and mental health by using this approach: As soon as they begin to saturate themselves with depression, go find someone for whom they can do something.

PEER SUPPORT TRAINING MODEL

The use of concern for others as a therapeutic resource can be expanded to a training model. With short-term preparation older persons should be able to be trained in the simple basic skills of human support procedures outlined in this book. This would prepare them to relate effectively to other older persons in emotional crises. Quite often the elderly complain that counselors and therapists who work with them are too young to understand what it means to be old. Trained older persons can counter this objection. Further, the economic problem of supporting enough professional counselors to meet the needs of a growing number of elderly could be largely solved by training the elderly themselves. Many counselors who are in the business prefer to work with younger clients with whom greater growth possibilities exist. Older persons, with training, by virtue of their cohort identification, will have a greater desire to work therapeutically with their peers.

The peer support training model will become more attractive as the counseling needs and possibilities of the elderly become more obvious. Having the elderly trained to work in teams of two will give them more confidence as they serve their own cohorts.

Nursing homes could train those residents who were willing to volunteer. They would be enormous support to an overworked staff. Self-confidence and prolonged independence of the elderly involved in the support teams would have significant reinforcement. Senior citizen centers, nutrition sites, family service organizations, and other agencies serving the elderly could train groups of their older participants to work with those older individuals having emotional and behavioral difficulties.

SUMMARY

The group structures available for reinforcing freedom and independence among the elderly offer more excitement for the later stages of the life cycle. The wing or floor assembly can revitalize the depressing atmosphere of most dependence-oriented nursing homes. For spouses who live in their own homes the couple conference structures dignity and self-respect. When troubles are overwhelming, older persons—no matter what their residential living situation may be—can find therapeutic help by seeking out others who need care. The training model, built on the therapeutic resource of caring, offers untapped potential for older persons living in institutional settings as well as in their private residences.

There has been a need for the research and theoretical works in the past that have exposed the contribution society has played in undermining feelings of usefulness and worth among older persons. But to dwell on this negative stereotyping is to give it even more influence. The need today is to build on this information. Our creativity must be turned now toward developing resources for understanding and nurturing freedom, self-respect, confidence, and prolonged independence among older persons. That is the purpose of this book. It is a concept whose time has arrived, again.

Chapter 7
Summary

To bring an informed counseling strategy to this period of life, a total perspective of what it means to grow old is essential. Knowing the general historical attitudes toward the aged gives a more realistic interpretation of the present and a more rational expectation of the future. If the long view—that is, from the perspective of history—is taken, the temptation toward forecasting doom is resisted. Historically, the negative attitude toward aging, on a larger social scale, is a relatively recent development (beginning toward the end of the middle ages). This factor does not lessen society's current negative stereotyping of the aging, but knowing the attitudes have been different at periods of our past offers a more positive view of the future for change. Knowing the sociological function of negative stereotypes helps to diffuse their personal impact.

Being aware of the current demographic trends and their implications gives a hopeful perspective about the future. The proportion of elderly in the population has doubled 2.5 times since 1900. With the birthrate in the United States continuing to decline, the elderly will increasingly become a force to be reckoned with. It is inevitable. The elders will rise again! It is only a matter of time.

Awareness of which biological declines appear to affect independent functioning and to what extent is crucial for the counselor. The physical condition of the older person must be taken into account along with any expectation of independence that requires more physical exertion than previously experienced. Knowing which physiological declines are the most crucial and which can be developed enables the elderly person to weave a reasonable prescription for independence. The individual's potential for development makes more sense when it is realized that all discussion in texts like this of biological decline is spoken of in terms of statistical averages. The average means there are a lot of people above the average as well as below.

A social systems umbrella seems tailored for a theoretical basis for counseling older persons. Within this approach the contributions of many intervention strategies can be integrated. Old people live in social systems. The behavior of each member affects all the others. Even in institutional settings there are systems. The assembly model is an intervention process for such a larger social structure of elderly.

Such a variety of strategies presented offers a number of options for counseling within one overall theoretical framework. This approach is grounded in a fundamental respect for the individual, emphasizing belonging, individual choice, encouragement toward greater responsibility taking, participatory governance, and assertiveness (individual and group). It is applicable to elderly in independent residential settings as well as those in institutions.

This book is not intended to be the last word in counseling the elderly. It is meant to be a beginning. You will shape its future directions.

APPENDIX

Appendix
Reminiscence Exercises

1. Famous sayings (fill in the blank spaces):
   (1) Don't fire ______ you see the ______ of their eyes.
   (2) ______ heal thyself.
   (3) You may fire when ready ______.
   (4) I do not know what course others may take, but as for me, give me ______ or give me ______.
   (5) The battle of Waterloo was fought on the playing fields of ______.
   (6) We have nothing to fear ______ itself.
   (7) Remember the ______.
   (8) The ballgame is not over ______ the last man is ______.
   (9) The do ______ congress.
   (10) I have just begun to ______.
2. (1) How old would you guess your first-grade teacher was when you were in the first grade? (Please write her age in the space to the right.) Age ______
   (2) In what year did Columbus discover America? Year ______

(3) How old was your father when you first learned to read? Age ______
(4) How old would your mother be if she were alive today? Age ______
(5) How old would your father be if he were alive today? Add 100 and put the answer in the space to the right. Answer ______
(6) Please add all the numbers you have put in the spaces to the right. Total ______
(7) Now subtract the age you were when you left school. Age ______
Total Answer ______

3. Can you remember looking out your window when you were a child? Think for about two minutes about the things you could have seen when you were a child that you are not likely to see today. Try and see if you can list ten of them.
(1)
(2)
(3)
(4)
(5)
(6)
(7)
(8)
(9)
(10)

4. About 300 cars that used to be made in America are no longer made. Please list as many as you can that were made before 1940.
(1)
(2)
(3)
(4)
(5)
(6)
(7)
(8)
(9)
(10)
Now put a check beside the ones you could have bought with $2000.

5. Can you remember the name of the grocery store at which your family shopped when you were very young?
Name ______________________________

Can you remember some of the items that your mother asked you to buy at the grocery store? Please list them.

(1)
(2)
(3)
(4)
(5)
(6)
(7)
(8)
(9)
(10)

6. Can you remember what it cost to heat your home when you were young? Cost ______
   Heating bills have gone up a great deal the past 20 years.
   What would it cost to heat the same size home (you grew up in) today? Cost ______
7. Please fill in the following blanks:
   (1) How old were you when you first had a radio? Age ______
   (2) When you first saw a TV? Age ______
   (3) How old were you when you were married? Age ______
   (4) What year was the great depression? Year ______
   Please add all the numbers Total ______
   Now subtract 5 Total Answer ______
8. Can you remember sitting in your living room when you were a young child? Think for several minutes and try to remember any things that were smaller than 20 inches long and 20 inches wide. List as many as you can think of.
   (1)
   (2)
   (3)
   (4)
   (5)
   (6)
   (7)
   (8)
   (9)
   (10)
9. Add the following. Please limit yourself to two minutes.
   (1) The number of people in your family when you were living with your parents. ______ ______
   (2) The number in your family now. ______
   (3) The number of times you have been in the hospital. ______

(4) The number of rooms in the first building you lived in. ______
(5) The number of children in your first grade classroom. ______
Add these together Total ______

10. Make a list now of the social and economic problems of 1945.
    (1)
    (2)
    (3)
    (4)
    (5)
    (6)
    (7)
    (8)
    (9)
    (10)
11. You want to measure a room you lived in at least 20 years ago. Write down the width and length of that room.
    Width ______ feet
    Length ______ feet
    You have no yardstick, but see a ruler which has only 5 inches marked on it. How many times would a 5-inch ruler have to be used to get an exact measure of the dimensions you listed above?
    Width ______
    Length ______
12. Can you write out a simple recipe for a cake your mother served often?
    You have lost your measuring set and all you have left is a one-quarter-cup measure and a one-half-teaspoon measure. You don't want to guess the amount. Show how many times you have to fill *each* measure to get the measure your cake called for.
13. Can you draw a map of the route you took home when you were in the third grade?
14. Do you remember the name of the first person you had a date with? If so write the name.
    Name ______
    Where did you go? ______
    For how long? ______
15. Do you think young people today have more fun than they did when you were young? ______
    What types of things did young people do for fun at that time?
    ______
16. Have you ever seen a blimp? ______ If so, can you remember your feelings when you first saw one? ______

17. Can you remember the first fish you caught?
    (1) How large was it? Inches ______
    (2) What kind was it? Kind ______
    (3) Where did you catch it? Location ______
    (4) Can you remember how you felt when you caught that fish? ______

References

Abdo, E., Dills, J., Schectman, H., and Yarnish, M. Elderly women in institutions versus those in public housing: a comparison of personal and social adjustment. *Journal of the American Geriatrics Society* 21(2), 1973, 81–87.

Achenbaum, W. A. The adolescence of old age. In J. Hendricks and C. Hendricks. *Dimensions of aging: Readings.* Cambridge, Mass.: Winthrop Publishers, 1979.

Adler, A. *Understanding human nature.* New York: Greenberg, 1929.

Adler, A. *What life should mean to you.* London: G. Allen, 1931.

Alberti, R. E., and Emmons, M. L. *Your perfect right.* San Luis Obispo, Calif.: Impact Publishers, Inc., 1974.

Allred, G. H., *Mission for mother: Guiding the child.* Salt Lake City: Bookcraft, 1968.

Amulree, Lord. Sex and the elderly. *Practitioner* 172, 1954, 431–435.

Ansbacher, H. L., and Ansbacher, R. R. *The individual psychology of Alfred Adler.* New York: Basic Books, 1956.

Atchley, R. C. *The social forces in later life.* Belmont, Calif.: Wadsworth, 1972.

Atchley, R. C. *The social forces in later life: An introduction to social gerontology*, 2nd ed. Belmont, Calif.: Wadsworth, 1977.

Baltes, Paul B. Strategies for psychological intervention in old age: A symposium. *Gerontologist* 13, Spring 1973, 4–6.

Baltes, M. M., and Lascomb, S. L. Creating a healthy institutional environment for the elderly via behavior management. *International Journal of Nursing Studies* 12, 1975, 5–12.

Baltes, M. M., and Zerke, M. B. Independence training in nursing home residents, *Gerontologist* 16, October 1976, 428–432.

Barnes, J. A. Effects of reality orientation classroom on memory loss, confusion, and disorientation in geriatric patients, *Gerontologist* 14(2), 1974, 139–142.

Bayne, J. R. Environmental modification for the older person. *Gerontologist* 11(1), 1971, 314–317.

Bengston, V. L. Sex in nursing homes. *Medical Aspects of Human Sexuality* 9, 1975, 21.

Benjamin, Harry. Impotence and aging. *Sexology* 26, 1958, 238–243.

Berezin, M. A. Sex and old age: a review of the literature. *Journal of Geriatric Psychiatry* 2, 1969, 131–149.

Birren, J. *The psychology of aging*. Englewood Cliffs, N.J.: Prentice-Hall, 1964.

Blackman, G. J., and Silberman, A. *Modification of child and adolescent behavior*, 2nd ed. Belmont, Calif.: Wadsworth, 1975.

Botwinick, J. *Cognitive processes in maturity and old age*. New York: Springer, 1967.

Botwinick, J. *Aging and behavior*. New York: Springer, 1973.

Bowen, Murray. *Family therapy in clinical practice*. New York: Aronson, 1978.

Bowman, Karl M. The sex life of the aging individual. *Geriatrics*, 1954, 83–84.

Brody, Stanley. Comprehensive health care for the elderly: An analysis. In J. Hendricks and C. Hendricks. *Dimensions of aging: Readings*. Cambridge, Mass.: Winthrop Publishers, 1979.

Bromley, D. B. *The psychology of human aging*. Baltimore: Penguin Books, 1966.

Browne, L. J., and Ritter, J. I. Reality therapy for the geriatric psychiatric patient. *Perspectives in Psychiatric Care* 10(3), 1972, 135–139.

Buhler, C. The curve of life as studied in biographies. *Journal of Applied Psychology* 14, 1935, 406.

Burgess, R. L., Clark, R. N., and Hendee, V. C. An experimental analysis of anti-litter procedures. *Journal of Applied Behavior Analysis* 4, 1971, 71–75.

Butler, R. The responsibility of psychiatry to the elderly. *American Journal of Psychiatry* 127, 1971, 1080–1081.

Butler, R. N. The life review: an interpretation of reminiscence in the aged. *Psychiatry*, 1963, 67.

Butler, R. V. *Why survive: Being old in America*. New York: Harper & Row, 1975.

Cameron, Paul. The generation gap: Beliefs about sexuality and self-reported sexuality. *Developmental Psychology* 3(2), 1970, 272.

Carp, F. Senility or garden variety maladjustment. *Journal of Gerontology* 24(2), 1969, 203–209.

Cavan, R. S. Speculations on innovations to conventional marriage in old age. *Gerontologist* 13(4), 1973, 409–411.

Chien, Ching-Piao. Psychiatric treatment for geriatric patients: Pub or drug? *American Journal of Psychiatry*, 127, 1971, 1070–1075.

Christensen, C. V., and Gagon, J. H. Sexual behavior in a group of older women. *Journal of Gerontology* 20(3), 1965, 351–356.

Christensen, C. V., and Johnson, A. Sexual patterns in a group of older never-married women. *Journal of Geriatric Psychiatry* 6(1), 1973, 80–98.

Citrin, R. S., and Dixon, D. N. Reality orientation. *Gerontologist* 17, 1977, 39–43.

Claman, A. D. Panel discussion: Sexual difficulties after 50. *Canadian Medical Association Journal* 94(5), 1966, 207.

Coleman, P. G. Measuring reminiscence characteristics from conversation as adaptative features of old age. *Journal of Aging and Human Development* 5, 1974, 281–294.

Comfort, Alex. Sexuality and aging. *SIECUS Report* 4(6), July 1976.

Coulter, O. W. New hope for older mental patients. *Aging* 161, 1968, 3–12.

Cumming, J., and Cumming, E. *Ego and milieu.* New York: Atherton, 1962.

Dean, Stanley R. Sin and the senior citizen. *Journal of the American Geriatrics Society* 14, 1966, 935–938.

De Beauvoir, Simone. *The coming of age.* New York: Putnam, 1972.

DeVries, J. Tips on how to stay young. *Newsweek*, April 16, 1973, 93.

Dickenson, T. Celebrations. *Harpers*, June 1973, 4.

Dreikurs, Rudolph. How to get along with oneself. Unpublished paper. 1964.

Dreikurs, R., Gould, S., and Corsini, R. *The family council.* Chicago: Alfred Adler Institute, 1974.

Ellis, A., and Harper, R. A. *New guide to rational living.* North Hollywood, Calif.: Wilshire Book Company, 1976.

Elmore, J. L. Adaptation to aging. *Gerontologist* 10, Spring 1970, 50–53.

Felton, B., and Kahana, E. Adjustment and situationally-bound locus of control among institutionalized aged. *Journal of Gerontology* 29(3), 1974, 295–301.

Filer, R. N., and O'Connell, D. D. Motivation of aging persons. *Journal of Gerontology* 19, 1964, 15–22.

Fine, R. Psychoanalysis. In R. Corsini (Ed.), *Current psychotherapies.* Itasca, Ill.: F. E. Peacock Publishers, Inc., 1973, 1–34.

Finkle, Alex L. Sex problems in later years. *Medical Times* 95, 1967, 416–419.

Finkle, Alex L. Emotional quality and physical quantity of sexual activities in aging males. *Journal of Geriatric Psychiatry* 6(1), 1973, 70–79.

Finkle, A. L. et al. Sexual potency in aging males. *Journal of the American Medical Association* 170, 1959, 1391–1393.

Frankl, V. *Man's search for meaning.* Boston: Beacon Press, 1963.

Garfinkel, R. The reluctant therapist. *Gerontologist* 15(2), April 1975, 136–137.

Giordano, J., and Giordano, G. Overcoming resistance to change in custodial institutions. *Hospital and Community Psychiatry* 25(8), 1972, 520–524.

Glover, B. H. Sex counseling of the elderly. *Hospital Practice*, June 1977, 101–113.

Goldberg, H. L. Psychiatric consultation: A strategic service to nursing home staffs. *Gerontologist* 10, Autumn 1970, 221–224.

Goldstein, A. A critical appraisal of milieu therapy in a geriatric day hospital. *Journal of the American Geriatric Society* 19, 1971, 693–699.

Gottesman, L. E. Milieu treatment of the aged in institutions. *Gerontologist* 13, 1973, 23–26.

Gubrium, J. F., and Ksander, M. On multiple realities and reality orientation. *Gerontologist* 15, April 1975, 142–145.

Guillerme, J. *Longevity*. New York: Walker and Company, 1963.

Havinghurst, R. J. A social-psychological perspective on aging. *Gerontologist* 8, 1968, 67–71.

Havinghurst, R. J., and Glasser, R. An exploratory study of reminiscence. *Journal of Gerontology* 27, 1972, 235–253.

Heap, R. F., Boblitt, W. E., Moore, C. H., and Hord, J. E. Behavior-milieu therapy with chronic neuropsychiatric patients. *Journal of Abnormal Psychology* 76, 1970, 349–354.

Hendricks, J., and Hendricks, C. S. *Aging in mass society*. Cambridge, Mass.: Winthrop Publishers, 1977.

Hendricks, J., and Hendricks, C. *Dimensions of aging: Readings*. Cambridge, Mass.: Winthrop Publishers, 1979.

Henry, J. *Culture against man*. New York: Knopf, 1965.

Heumann, L. F. Planning assisted independent living programs for the semi-independent elderly. *Gerontologist* 18(2), 1978, 145–152.

Hickey, T. Psychologic rehabilitation for the "normal" elderly. *Mental Hygiene* 53, 1969, 364–374.

Hoyer, W. Application of operant techniques to the modification of elderly behavior. *Gerontologist* 13(1), Spring 1973, 18–22.

Hoyer, W. J., Kafer, R. A., Simpson S. C., and Hoyer, F. W. Reinstatement of verbal behavior in elderly mental patients using operant procedures. *Gerontologist* 14, 1974, 149–152.

Hughston, G. A. The effects of two educational interventions on the cognitive functioning of older people. Doctoral dissertation, Pennsylvania State University, University Park, Pa. 37(5), 1976.

Kantor, O., Hiller, A., and Thuell, J. Developing an activity program in a welfare hotel. *Hospital and Community Psychiatry* 25(8), 1974, 520–524.

Kassel, Victor. Polygymy after 60. *Geriatrics* 21(4), April 1966, 214–218.

Kassel, Victor. Sex and the elderly. *Psychology Today*, June 1974, 18.

Kastenbaum, R. The reluctant therapist. In R. Kastenbaum (Ed.), *New thoughts on old age*. New York: Springer, 1964.

Keller, J. F., Brooking, J. Y., and Croake, J. Effects of a program in rational thinking on anxiety in older persons. *Journal of Counseling Psychology* 22, 1975, 54–57.

Kimmel, Douglas C. *Adulthood and aging: an interdisciplinary developmental view.* New York: Wiley, 1974.

Kinch, R. A. H. Sexual difficulties after 50: The gynecologists' view. *Canadian Medical Association Journal* 94, January 29, 1966, 211–212.

Kleemeier, R. W., Ed. *Aging and leisure.* New York: Oxford University Press, 1961.

Knox, D. *Dr. Knox's marital exercise book.* New York: McKay, 1975.

LeCompte, W. F., and Williams, E. P. Ecological analysis of a hospital. In J. Archea and C. Eastman (Eds.), *EDRA-2: Proceedings of the Second Annual Environmental Design Research Association Conference.* Pittsburgh: Carnegie Press, 1970.

Lederer, W. J., and Jackson, D. *The mirages of marriage.* New York: Norton, 1968.

Levin, Sidney. Some comments on the distribution of narcissists and object libido in the aged. *International J. of Psycho-analysis* 46, 1965, 200–208.

Lewis, C. N. Reminiscing and self-concept in old age. *Human Development* 17, 1971, 259–272.

Lieberman, M. A., and Falk, J. M. The remembered past as a source of data for research on the life cycle. *Human Development* 14, 1971, 132–141.

Lorenze, E. J. Physical activity and aging. In L. E. Brown and E. O. Ellis (Eds.), *Quality of life.* Acton, Mass.: Publishing Sciences Group, Inc., 1975, 93–100.

Love, Nash. Personal correspondence, 1976.

Lowman, W. *Family constellation: its effects on personality and social behavior*, 3rd rev. ed. New York: Springer, 1976.

McClannahan, L. E., and Risley, T. V. Design of living environments for nursing home residents: Increasing participation in recreation activities. *Journal of Applied Behavior Analysis* 8, 1975, 261–268.

McDonald, M. L., and Butler, A. K. Reversal of helplessness: producing walking behavior in nursing home wheelchair residents using behavior modification procedures. *Journal of Gerontology* 29, 1974, 97–101.

McMahon, A. W., Jr., and Rhudick, P. J. Reminiscing in the aged: an adaptational response. In S. Levin and R. J. Kahana (Eds.), *Psychodynamic studies on aging: Creativity, reminiscing, and dying.* New York: International Universities Press, 1967.

Minuchin, S. *Families and family therapy.* Cambridge, Mass.: Harvard University Press, 1974.

Minuchin, S. et al. A conceptual model of psychosomatic illness in children. *Archives of General Psychiatry* 32, August 1975, 1031–1038.

Mosak, H., and Dreikurs, R. Adlerian psychotherapy. In R. Corsini (Ed.), *Current psychotherapies.* Itasca, Ill.: Peacock Publishers, Inc., 1973.

Neugarten, B. A developmental view of the adult personality. In J. E. Birren (Ed.), *Relations of development and aging.* Springfield, Ill.: Thomas, 1964.

Neugarten, B. Age groups in American society and the rise of the young old.

Annals of the American Academy of Political and Social Sciences 415, September 1974.

Newsweek. The graying of America, February 28, 1977.

Nikelly, A. *Techniques for behavior change*. Springfield, Ill.: Thomas, 1971.

Otto, H. A., Ed. *Exploration in human potentialities*. Springfield, Ill.: Thomas, 1966.

Patterson, R. D. Servers for the aged in community mental health centers. *American Journal of Psychiatry* 133(3), March 1976, 271–273.

Pfeiffer, Eric. Geriatric sex behavior. *Medical Aspects of Human Sexuality* 3(7), 1969, 19–28.

Pfeiffer, Eric, and Davis, Glenn C. Determinants of sexual behavior in middle and old age. *Journal of the American Geriatrics Society* 20(4), 1972, 151–158.

Pfeiffer, E., and Davis, G. C. Determinants of sexual behavior in middle and old age. *Normal aging II*. Durham, N.C.: Duke University Press, 1974.

Pfeiffer, E., Verwoerdt, A., and Davis, G. C. *Sexual behavior in middle life. Normal aging II*. Durham, N.C.: Duke University Press, 1974, 243–251.

Pressey, S. L., and Pressey, A. D. Major neglected need opportunity: Old age counseling. *Journal of Counseling Psychology* 19(5), 1972, 362–366.

Rathbone-McCuan, E., and Levenson, J. Impact of socialization therapy in a geriatric day-care setting. *Gerontologist* 15(4), August 1975, 338–342.

Rebok, G. W., and Hoyer, W. J. The functional context of elderly behavior. *Gerontologist* 17, February 1977, 27–34.

Reichard, S., Livson, F., and Peterson, P. G. *Aging and personality*. New York: Wiley, 1962.

Rodstein, M., Savitsky, E., and Starkman, R. Initial adjustment to a long-term care institution: Medical and behavioral aspects. *Journal of the American Geriatrics Society* 24(1), 1976, 65–71.

Romney, L. Community action and self help: Tools for purposeful living. *Nursing Homes* 19, March 1970, 32–35.

Sanders, R., Smith, R. S., and Weinman, W. S. *Chronic psychosis and recovery*. San Francisco: Jossey-Bass, 1967.

Satchell, M. How to enjoy life—up to the last moment. *Parade*, October 16, 1977, 23–24.

Schaie, K. W. Age changes in adult intelligence. In D. S. Woodruff and J. E. Birren, *Aging*. New York: Van Nostrand, 1975, 111–124.

Sinex, Marrott. Biochemistry of aging. In M. G. Spencer and C. J. Dorr (Eds.), *Understanding aging: A multidisciplinary approach*. New York: Appleton, 1975.

Steer, R., and Boger, W. P. Milieu therapy with psychiatric-medically infirm patients. *Gerontologist* 15(2), April 1975, 138–141.

Stephens, L. P. *Reality orientation*. Washington, D.C.: American Psychiatric Association, 1969.

Swartz, David. Sexual difficulties after 50: The urologists' view. *Canadian Medical Association Journal* 94, Jauuary 29, 1966, 208–210.

Taylor, Charles. Creativity throughout the life span. Issues of Concern in Gerontology Conference, Virginia Polytechnic Institute and State University, Blacksburg, Virginia, January 25–26, 1977.

Toman, W. *Family constellation.* New York: Springer, 1976.

Turbow, S. R. Geriatric group day care and its effects on independent living. *Gerontologist* 15(6), December 1975, 508–510.

Verwoerdt, Adrian. Sexual behavior in senescence: Patterns of sexual activity and interest. *Geriatrics* 24(2), February 1969, 137–154.

Verwoerdt, A., Pfeiffer, T., and Hscah-Shan Wang. Several behaviors in senescence, changes in sexual activities and interest in aging men and women. *Journal of Geriatric Psychiatry* 1 & 2, 1967, 163–180.

Wahler, R. G. Some structural aspects of deviant child behavior. *Journal of Applied Behavior Analysis* 8, 1975, 27–42.

Weg, Ruth. Changing physiology of aging: Normal and pathological. In D. S. Woodruff and J. E. Birren, *Aging.* New York: Van Nostrand, 1975.

Weg, R. Personal communication, August 1976.

Woodruff, D. S., and Birren, J. E. *Aging: Scientific perspectives and social issues.* New York: Van Nostrand, 1975.

Index

80 81 82 9 8 7 6 5 4 3 2 1